T0312306

Cambridge Elements ≡

Elements in Language Teaching
edited by
Heath Rose
Linacre College, University of Oxford
Jim McKinley
University College London

REFLECTIVE PRACTICE IN LANGUAGE TEACHING

Thomas S. C. Farrell
Brock University

CAMBRIDGE
UNIVERSITY PRESS

CAMBRIDGE
UNIVERSITY PRESS

University Printing House, Cambridge CB2 8BS, United Kingdom

One Liberty Plaza, 20th Floor, New York, NY 10006, USA

477 Williamstown Road, Port Melbourne, VIC 3207, Australia

314–321, 3rd Floor, Plot 3, Splendor Forum, Jasola District Centre,
New Delhi – 110025, India

103 Penang Road, #05–06/07, Visioncrest Commercial, Singapore 238467

Cambridge University Press is part of the University of Cambridge.

It furthers the University's mission by disseminating knowledge in the pursuit of
education, learning, and research at the highest international levels of excellence.

www.cambridge.org
Information on this title: www.cambridge.org/9781009013901
DOI: 10.1017/9781009028783

© Thomas S. C. Farrell 2022

First published 2022

A catalogue record for this publication is available from the British Library.

ISBN 978-1-009-01390-1 Paperback
ISSN 2632-4415 (online)
ISSN 2632-4407 (print)

Reflective Practice in Language Teaching

Elements in Language Teaching

DOI: 10.1017/9781009028783
First published online: April 2022

Thomas S. C. Farrell
Brock University
Author for correspondence: Thomas S. C. Farrell, tfarrell@brocku.ca

Abstract: This Element examines the concept of reflective practice in language teaching, reconsidering a framework for a holistic approach to language teacher reflection and reflective practice. It includes a brief description of reflective practice and how it is operationalized by two of its main protagonists, John Dewey and Donald Schön, as well as some of the limitations of their conceptions. This Element is used as an introduction to how the author developed Dewey and Schön's ideas when creating a five-stage framework of reflective practice for language teachers. The author then presents an in-depth case study of the reflections of an English as a foreign language (EFL) teacher working in Costa Rica as he moved through the five stages of the framework. The author then outlines and discusses how reflective practice may be moved forward and calls attention to the importance of emotions in the process of reflection for language teachers.

Keywords: reflective teaching, language teaching, language teachers, John Dewey, Donald Schön

ISBNs: 9781009013901 (PB), 9781009028783 (OC)
ISSNs: 2632-4415 (online), 2632-4407 (print)

Contents

1 Background

The overall goal of this Element is to provide a comprehensive argument for reconsidering a framework I devised (Farrell, 2015) for a five-stage approach to language teacher reflective practice, supported by an in-depth case study I conducted in which I added appraisal analysis to the framework. Uncertainty over the meaning of reflection and reflective practice is due to the majority of recent approaches having been based on an understanding (which is most likely a misunderstanding) of the two most popularly cited theoretical sources, namely the works of John Dewey and Donald Schön. One of the aims of this Element is to return to these two theoretical sources in order to clarify what I mean by the notion of reflective practice and then to establish the criteria (i.e., framework) I use to clearly define what I mean by reflective practice for language teachers. I add another dimension, the emotional aspect of reflection, related to reflective teaching within my framework. As Fook (2010) has noted, emotions can not only trigger learning issues for teachers but can also act as an "impetus and motivation for finding meaning and continuing reflection" (p. 48). This Element goes on to consider how, in my own work, I have built on some of the limitations or constraints in the work of Dewey and Schön in the development of what I have referred to as a holistic approach to reflective practice for language teachers (Farrell, 2015).

1.1 Organization of This Element

In this first section, I introduce the topics of reflective practice and reflection. I briefly outline where the concept of reflection originated and examine some of the main issues associated with the uncertainty around how it has been understood. I then connect these issues with an argument for the need to reconceptualize reflective practice in language education. From here, I close the section with an attempt to disentangle the different terms related to reflection and reflective practice to bring clarity to the concepts.

In Section 2, I first examine the theoretical underpinnings, both the perspectives and the constraints, of the models of reflection presented by both Dewey and Schön – two of the most generally uncritically incorporated sources of inspiration language teacher educators and language teachers use to justify their reflection within language teaching (Farrell, 2018). In this light, I follow the discussion of the theoretical underpinnings with an overview of the development of my own framework (Farrell, 2015) and an explanation of how the framework was designed especially for language teachers to reflect on practice, and how this has been developed from the work of Dewey, Schön, and others.

In Section 3, I outline and discuss how I used my framework in a recent in-depth case study with one English as a foreign language (EFL) teacher in Costa Rica as he reflected intensely on his work over a two-month period during the height of the COVID-19 pandemic when he was suddenly required to teach all his classes on an online platform (Zoom). In this section, I give details about how Damien (pseudonym) reflected on his philosophy, principles, theory, practice, and beyond (Farrell, 2015). I also outline and discuss how I applied the Appraisal Framework from systemic functional linguistics (SFL) with a specific focus on the aspect of affect to account for the range of emotive language Damien used when reflecting. This latter analysis is a new addition to the framework for reflecting on practice, and I believe it is a promising tool for future researchers, language teacher educators, and language teachers for gauging the importance of emotions within the process of reflective teaching.

In Section 4, I consider how the concept of reflective practice can be moved forward in language teaching. Section 5 brings a conclusion to this Element. One final point to emphasize is that the focus is on how to encourage language teachers to reflect on themselves and their practices both inside and outside the classroom as part of their professional development. (I use the term *language teaching* to include the field of teaching English to speakers of other languages [TESOL] that includes EFL and English as a second language [ESL] teachers. This Element does not cover second language students or student learning and reflection; rather, it covers the education of second language teachers and getting them to reflect.)

1.2 Reflective Practice and Reflection

Reflective practice as a mark of professional competence has taken hold across many professions in recent times (e.g., science, law, medicine, nursing, and education). For example, reflective practice has been cited as especially helpful for students of law who lack practical experience because they can, as Anzalone (2010) has noted, "examine and test beliefs and principles against what is being learned doctrinally" (p. 86). Within the nursing profession, reflective practice has been cited as an important concept because it can help narrow the divide between theory and practice (Kim et al., 2010). Within the field of education, as Tabachnik and Zeichner (2002) have pointed out, "there is not a single teacher educator who would say that he or she is not concerned about preparing teachers who are reflective" (p. 13).

Thus, reflective practice has taken a firm hold within teacher preparation and development programs as an essential skill (Loughran, 2002; Lytle & Cochran-Smith, 1992). Reflective practice offers teachers a way to articulate those aspects of practice that make up part of that knowledge base in teaching by helping practitioners better understand what they know and do as they (re) consider what they learn in and through their teaching (Smyth, 1992). As Zwozdiak-Myers (2012, p. 3) has pointed out, reflective practice is central to a teacher's development because it helps teachers "analyse and evaluate what is happening" in their classes so they can not only improve the quality of their teaching but also provide better learning opportunities for their students.

Within language teaching, reflective practice has also arguably become an even more important concept as the profession has moved into a "post-method condition" (Kumaravadivelu, 2003) where language teachers no longer rely on prescribed teaching methods. Generally, reflective practice for language teachers, as Freeman (2016) puts it, is the "mental activity that teachers do as they think in teaching situations" (p. 207). Its inclusion in language teacher education and development programs, according to Freeman, is based on two premises: "(1) Improvement in teaching comes when teachers can turn actions that are automatic and routine into ones that are considered. (2) This shift from automatic to considered actions supports a more professionalized view of teaching" (p. 221). Thus, although reflective practice has been embraced enthusiastically in recent years in the field of language teaching, "what it actually is and how it might be developed are more problematic" (Walsh & Mann, 2015, p. 351).

In other words, although reflection and reflective practice have gained prominence in language teaching as marks of professional competence, and reflective practice has been considered a significant component of many preservice language teacher education and in-service development programs, there is still little agreement about how to define the concept or indeed what strategies can operationalize or promote reflective teaching. Thus, although most language educators still concur that some form of reflection is desirable for language teachers, the precise definition of reflective practice remains vague, with resulting misunderstandings about the philosophical traditions behind whose work is most cited when attempting to define and operationalize this interesting yet complex topic.

The concept of reflection can be traced back to various ancient and current religions, but the current use of the term *reflection* comes from the Latin word *reflectere* and means "to bend back" (Valli, 1997, p. 67) or to look back and become more aware of a past event or issue. From ancient historical cultural and religious roots (e.g., ancient Greece, China, and India) we recognize that humans tend to "reflect" in some manner as they go about their daily lives. In the early twentieth century, reflection and reflective practice appeared especially in North America through the seminal work of John Dewey. Dewey

(1933) was initially interested in encouraging more reflection in student learning (rather than with teachers) because he worried that routine thinking and decision-making by students in educational settings would not lead to a complete education. He extended this idea of *reflective inquiry* to teachers on the basis of noting that teachers who do not reflect on their work can become slaves to routine because their actions are guided mostly by impulse, tradition, and/or authority rather than by informed decision-making. This decision-making, Dewey (1933) insisted, should be based on systematic and conscious reflections because teaching experience, when combined with these reflections, can lead to awareness, development, and growth.

Thus, Dewey (1933) maintained that reflective practice entails "active, persistent, and careful consideration of any belief or supposed form of knowledge in light of the grounds that support it and the further consequences to which it leads" (p. 9). This famous and often used quote has proved to be the basis of many subsequent approaches to reflection and reflective practice, and the concept saw a resurgence in the 1980s with the work of Donald Schön (1983, 1987). Whereas Dewey (1933) encouraged practitioners to reflect after the action, or "reflection-*on*-action," Schön (1983, 1987) encouraged practitioners to reflect during action, or "reflection-*in*-action," on the basis that practitioners can see more than they can explain. Schön wanted to encourage practitioners to reflect as they engaged in this action (I explain this in more detail section 2 below).

1.3 Reconceptualizing Reflective Practice in Language Education

Herein lies one of the major issues related to many previous discussions and implementations of reflective practice in language education. Both Dewey's (1933) oft-cited definition and his overall "reflection-on-action" approach, as well as the frequent references to and citations of Schön's (who incidentally did not work much with teachers) "reflection-in-action" approach, have been used in the scholarly literature in language education without any real critical examination. This has resulted in concealing the exact nature of reflection and its implications for language teacher education and language teaching. For example, in their probing article on "doing reflective practice" within language education, Walsh and Mann (2015) noted that the many challenges regarding understanding the true nature of reflective practice can make operationalizing reflective practice difficult for researchers and language teachers alike; as Walsh and Mann (2015) stated, "the many differing (and even conflicting) perspectives on what reflection actually means make it difficult for researchers and practitioners to operationalize it in any meaningful way" (p. 215). For instance, when language teacher candidates or experienced language teachers are encouraged to reflect, it is important to know in whose tradition this reflection is mirrored and how reflection is operationalized based on the underlying traditions. Within language teaching, then, as Freeman (2016) maintains, although reflective practice can offer a way into the "less accessible aspects of [a language] teacher's work" (p. 208), this access really depends on how reflection is operationalized.

Essentially, I suggest that one of the main reasons scholars and practitioners alike have problems with "doing" reflective practice is a lack of understanding of what reflective practice is and how it can be operationalized in language teaching; thus, there is confusion about the nature of reflection for teachers and teacher educators. As Freeman (2016) asks, "is 'reflection' a clearly defined concept or has it become a catch-all?" (p. 208).

As Freeman (2016) observed, "conceptualizing reflection in teaching is usually traced back to the work of John Dewey [and] Donald Schön on whose work the notion of reflection in education largely rests" (p. 208). However, both offer very different models of reflective practice and both are limited. Thus, in the spirit of reflective practice, in what follows, I examine both of their models because both have been very influential to my own work but also different to my approach.

1.4 Disentangling the Terms

Having provided a brief overview of the top topic and argument of this Element, I now briefly summarize some of the key terms related to reflection and reflective practice in language teaching to show why there seems to be so much confusion with how they are used in the literature.

In any review of the literature on reflective teaching, it is possible to find terms that vary in meaning, and sometimes it is difficult to unravel them. Within the field of language teaching, I (2018) recently extensively reviewed research on the practices that encourage ESL and EFL teachers to reflect on their own practices. Of the 138 studies published in academic peer-reviewed journals (I did not include monographs, book chapters, or books on reflective practice) over a seven-year period (2009–2015), I noted that only 52 of those studies attempted to define reflective practice (with citations). Furthermore, only 11 of the 52 studies attempted to define or very loosely defined the concept by just citing scholars' work. Seventy-five studies (or more than 50 percent of the total) did not give any definition of the concept but led into a discussion of "reflective practice" without saying what it was. Indeed, many studies used different terms such as *reflection, reflective practice, critical reflection, reflective teaching, reflective action, reflection-in-action, reflection-on-action, reflective practitioner, reflective thinking, reflective inquiry, analytical reflection*, and so on interactively in the sense that they had the same meaning as *reflection* or *reflective practice*. As I remarked, this lack of clarity around the overall concept of reflection and reflective practice and related terms is problematic within language teaching. Lack of clarity with regard to what we mean by reflection and lack of understanding of models of knowledge that underpin reflective practice make it difficult to operationalize the concept.

In addition, I (2018) discovered that, of the citations from the 52 studies (out of 138) that actually defined reflective practice in TESOL, the "main" scholars outside language teaching who were cited as a source for the research included Dewey (19 citations) and Schön (22 citations), and most of these only provided a quotation from either Dewey or Schön to legitimize their particular approach, perhaps without a full understanding of their approaches and theoretical grounding.

Within language teaching, early incorporation of the term *reflection* distinguished between a "weak" form and a "strong" form. In its weakest version, reflection was said to be no more than "thoughtful" practice where language teachers sometimes, as Wallace (1996) suggested, "informally evaluate various aspects of their professional expertise" (p. 292). However, as Wallace also pointed out, this type of "informal reflection" does not really lead to improved teaching and can even lead to more "unpleasant emotions without suggesting any way forward" (p. 13). Thus, a second, "stronger" form of or stance on reflection in language teaching emerged that proposed that language teachers should systematically collect data about their teaching and use that information to make responsible decisions about their teaching (Richards & Lockhart, 1994). In fact, this stance on reflection reiterates what Dewey (1933) noted about reflection when he said that "data (facts) and ideas (suggestions, possible solutions) thus form the two indispensable and correlative factors of all reflective activity" (p. 104). In more recent discussions on reflection in language teaching, Walsh and Mann (2015) have echoed this call for data-led reflective practice by encouraging teachers to collect data as a concrete means of focusing their reflections so they can make more insightful analysis and gain a fuller sense of their own teaching.

Recently, this second, "stronger" conceptualization of reflection is beginning to take hold within language teaching (e.g., see Mann & Walsh, 2017, for an excellent analysis and implementation of evidence-based reflective practice for language teachers). Nevertheless, we must still be careful that evidence-based approaches are not reduced solely to solving teaching problems that have occurred in class, where teachers are encouraged to collect data to "fix" classroom problems without any critical reflection on the social, affective, moral, or political aspects related to practice. Indeed, we must also be careful that critical reflections on practice consist of more than asking why a teacher uses a particular method in a lesson, as occurred within the early literature on reflection in the field of language teaching; as Hatton and Smith (1995) also noted many years ago, there is such a problem with the term *critical reflection*. They observed that some take it to "mean no more than constructive self-criticism of one's actions with a view to improvement" (p. 35).

In order to critically reflect on our practices, we must move beyond self-critical conceptual descriptions and examine the ideological influences that impact these practices as well as consider the interplay between our emotions and our reflections. One early notable exception within the field of language teaching who advocated for such a critical approach was Bartlett (1990), who maintained that we include the broader society in any approaches to reflections on teaching. Bartlett noted that critically reflective teachers must "transcend the technicalities of teaching and think beyond the need to improve . . . instructional techniques" (p. 204). However, Bartlett's ideas were largely ignored within language teaching until scholars such as Crookes (2013) wanted a more critical approach and advocated "teaching for social justice, in ways that support the development of active, engaged citizens who . . . will be prepared to seek out solutions to the problems they define and encounter, and take action accord-ingly" (p. 8). Thus, reflection should also include language teachers reflecting on the equitable nature of the profession (Hatton & Smith, 1995), as well as critically reflecting on the presence of power structures within the institutions in which they work (Brookfield, 1995).[1]

The problems of unraveling the semantics of the terms *reflection* and *reflect-ive practice* outlined earlier in this Element also include the place and meaning of the term *reflexive* as in "reflexive practice." Coghlan and Brannick (2005) maintain that "reflexivity is the constant analysis of one's own theoretical and methodological presuppositions" (p. 6). Within language teaching, Edge (2011) contends, the term *reflexive* overlaps and interacts with reflection and reflective practice. However, one major difference I see is that the term *reflexive practice* denotes a more inward-looking, individual reflective activity where practi-tioners look at their own self-trajectories, which for the most part are discon-nected from others; indeed, as Edge acknowledges, "the reflexive invites the autobiographical" (p. 25). I agree that language teachers and language teacher educators should interrogate their own philosophies, principles, theories, and

---

[1] I return to the issue of critical reflection in Section 2.2 when I outline and discuss my framework for reflecting on practice, as it includes coverage of critical reflection that I call "beyond practice," and how I specifically attempt to integrate teacher emotions within the framework as an integral aspect of reflective teaching.

practices and critically reflect beyond practice; however, I also agree with Dewey (1933), who maintained that the process is social and as a result, it is best carried out in the presence of others. Thus, my framework for reflecting on practice outlined in this Element is both "reflective" and "reflexive"; as Thompson and Pascal (2012) pointed out, the former incorporates the more "traditional notion of reflection as an analytical process" and the latter, reflexive approach emphasizes "the mirroring of practice, and thereby undertaking a self-analysis" (p. 320).

Note that, because of word count restrictions, this Element cannot and does not attempt to review all the literature related to all the different definitions of or approaches to reflective practice (but see Farrell, 2017, for a detailed outline of how language teacher educators attempted to incorporate some kind of reflection within their language teacher education programs in order to bridge the theory/practice divide they noticed between the content of their courses and the reality of the classroom; Farrell, 2018, for a report on the research conducted on reflective practice; and Farrell, 2019a, for an analysis of the different typologies of and approaches to reflective practice). Rather, I only focus on the two most cited approaches from Dewey and Schön and their influence in the development of my own framework.

2 "Standing on the Shoulders of Giants": Dewey and Schön

My own interest in the concept of reflective practice is long-standing (e.g., Farrell, 1999a, 1999b, 2001, 2004, 2006, 2007, 2008, 2013a, 2013b, 2014, 2016). Throughout its early period, my work was influenced by Dewey and Schön as two scholar giants. However, I was not fully convinced of the efficacy of their approaches beyond their pragmatic attraction when it came to implementing reflective practice. About ten years ago, I endeavored to reflect on reflective practice after working with this concept for more than ten years before that (including completing my PhD dissertation on the topic) but never questioning why I was so influenced by these scholars nor what exactly their approaches stood for. Now it seems almost mandatory to cite both scholars but without full knowledge of what they really represent. Indeed, within language teacher education, a recent review of an edited book that included the topic of reflection critically noted that the mandatory citation of Schön's work was somehow missing (Ur, 2020). However, while I fully acknowledge that Schön's work on reflective teaching is very important, merely citing his and Dewey's work is not a sufficient justification for their inclusion because, as Hébert (2015) suggests, we also need to better understand the intricacies of their approaches. Thus, my aim in this section is to point out that teacher educators, researchers, and language teachers should not uncritically pay "homage" to their work without a full understanding of what their work means within reflective practice.

It is also because of their huge influence on the development of my own framework that it encourages language teachers to reflect on their teaching. It is important for language teachers, teacher educators, researchers, and policy makers who may want to operationalize reflective teaching based on citing these almost "canonical" sources (Hébert, 2015) to have a clear understanding of the underlying theoretical traditions. One important reason for seeking such clarity is that when preservice and/or in-service language teachers are asked to reflect within language teacher education and development programs, more attention should be afforded to discussions about whose ideological tradition this request mirrors (Collin, Karsenti, & Komis, 2013; Hébert, 2015). Indeed, Hébert has suggested that, in order to retain the spirit of reflection, all models should be "critically examined and their connection to Dewey and Schön closely scrutinized" (p. 362). Akbari (2007) noted, "it is good to reflect, but reflection itself also requires reflection" (p. 205).

2.1 Dewey and Schön: Perspectives and Constraints

2.1.1 Perspectives

Dewey's (1933) main approach to reflective practice is called *reflective inquiry*, where he suggests practitioners can slow down the interval between thought and action as they pass through its five main phases of reflection. The first phase is called *suggestion*, where a practitioner faces a problematic issue and quickly comes up with some vague suggestions as possible solutions. Here Dewey (1933) maintains that practitioners suspend immediate judgment to consider alternative reasons for the problem as they move into the second phase, called *intellectualization*. During this phase, the practitioner's initial emotional reaction is converted into an intellectual reaction as he or she moves from problem "felt" to problem to be solved. The practitioner begins to refine the problem by asking more probing questions; as Dewey (1933) noted, a question well asked is half the answer already. The third phase is called *guiding idea*, where the practitioner gathers as much information about the problem as possible from as many different sources as possible in order to come up with a working hypothesis. Indeed, during this third phase, I have encouraged language teachers to also consider Brookfield's (1995) idea of looking at a problem through different lenses – the teacher's lens, the colleague's lens, the student's lens, and a literature review lens – in order to gather as much information as possible about the problem at hand. The fourth phase is called *reasoning*, and here the practitioner attempts to come up with a tentative solution based on all the information gathered thus far. The practitioner makes a tentative plan that he or she does not know will work at that time when he or she moves into the fifth and final phase, called *hypothesis testing*. After deciding the plan, the practitioner tests it by action and observation to see if it works; if it does not work, the practitioner attempts to generate different solutions and test these in a similar manner. The approach combines his or her process approach with the product approach to reflection; the process begins when a problematic issue arises which he or she calls "suggestion" in the first phase of the model. The product of reflection is solving the problem, ideally at the end of phase five.

Although I present the reflective inquiry phases in linear fashion, Dewey acknowledged that teachers do not (and probably should not) go through each of these phases in a lockstep fashion. Dewey also recognized that going through the process of reflective inquiry is not easy, because reflective thinking involves suspending immediate judgment so that we can delay reaching hasty conclusions. Thus, Dewey (1933) was encouraging teachers to take a step back by going through all the phases and to avoid jumping to early conclusions before having had an opportunity to examine the issue or problem in detail.

Dewey's (1933) approach to reflection has had immense influence on the work of other scholars over the intervening years who have since built on this model. For example, Boud, Keogh, and Walker (1985) have suggested a more cyclical model with three broader categories of reflective thought (experience, reflection, and outcome) that also emphasizes emotion as an element of reflective practice. In addition, Zeichner and Liston (1996, 2014) also returned to Dewey's (1933) original ideas when they distinguished between routine action and reflective action and suggested that, for teachers, "routine action is guided primarily by tradition, external authority and circumstance," whereas reflective action "entails the active, persistent and careful consideration of any belief or supposed form of knowledge" (Zeichner & Liston, 1996, p. 24). In addition, Jay and Johnson (2002) use Dewey's (1933) description of reflection as "the active, persistent, and careful consideration of any belief or supposed form of knowledge in light of the grounds that support it" (p. 9). Indeed, I believe that Dewey's (1933) evidence-based reflective inquiry cycle is most likely a precursor to action research steps that have been incorporated in general education and language teaching in modern times (e.g., Burns, 2010).

In addition, Dewey (1933) noted that knowledge of the strategies and methods of reflective practice are not enough by themselves because "there must be the desire, the will, to employ them. This is an affair of personal disposition" (p. 30). Thus, Dewey (1933) maintained that reflection needs to be guided by a set of attitudes to make the reflection truly meaningful. Dewey

(1933) pointed out that the mark of an intellectually educated person is the development of such attitudes or habits but that they do not come naturally and so must be acquired through training. Dewey maintained that in order to be considered truly reflective, teachers must cultivate (at least) three attitudes: being open-minded, responsible, and wholehearted.

Dewey (1933) defined the attitude of open-mindedness as "freedom from prejudice, partisanship, and such other habits as close the mind and make it unwilling to consider new problems and entertain new ideas" (p. 136). Open-mindedness suggests that we need to "let go" of being right all the time and that we should question our thinking and doubts in a kind of self-observation in order to gain more insight into our actions, thoughts, and learning, or to "admit that a belief to which we have once committed ourselves is wrong" (p. 136). To be truly open-minded one must, as Dewey pointed out, be willing to listen to all sides as well as to note all the facts from different sources and be open to looking into alternative solutions even if one has to admit one was not correct in the first instance.

The attitude of being responsible is connected to being open-minded in that Dewey encouraged practitioners to consider the consequences of whatever actions they adopt as a result of changing their beliefs. As Dewey (1933) noted, a responsible attitude is one where people "consider the consequences of a projected step," which means "to be willing to adopt these consequences when they follow reasonably from any position already taken" (p. 138). However, he noted that it is not uncommon for practitioners to continue to hold onto false beliefs, because they are unable or unwilling to accept the consequences and, as a result, may not be able to compete any project.

When a reflective practitioner is wholehearted – the third attitude – he or she must take up any project with a "whole heart" by committing fully to reflection. Dewey (1933) pointed out that "there is no greater enemy of effective thinking than divided interest"; nevertheless, he noted that when practitioners are fully invested, the issue at hand will sustain their reflections. In other words, reflective teachers have a wholehearted attitude they will reflect throughout their careers. I include much of Dewey's ideas in my own definition of reflective practice.

There was a lull for many years after Dewey's significant contribution of the concept of reflection in education (and what some would suggest could be called revolutionary thoughts on the need for both students and teachers to reflect on their practices). This was until the 1980s with the emergence of the work of Donald Schön (1983, 1987). Some scholars maintain that imprints of Dewey's work are ever present in the work of Schön, and in fact, Schön's PhD dissertation (Yale, philosophy, 1955) was focused on an analysis of Dewey's "Theory of

Inquiry." Although Schön did not refer to Dewey much in his work, I believe Dewey's philosophical pragmatism and influence led him to take a more pragmatic (rather than theoretical) approach to reflective practice (which also attracted me to his work).

Most of Schön's initial work was within organizations in terms of how practitioners in these organizations viewed their work, and especially the notion of practitioner-generated intuitive practice. Schön (1983) made this clear in his early influential book, *The Reflective Practitioner: How Professionals Think in Action*, when he noted the need for a greater understanding of the knowledge of practitioners as they practice.

In the 1970s, while at MIT, Schön teamed up with Chris Argyris and developed the (now famous) notion of single-loop and double-loop learning, where thinking, practice, and problems between the two are raised to an explicit level (rather than remaining at the usual tacit level) where they can be accessed (Argyris & Schön, 1974). This collaboration with Argyris led him to focus on professional learning within organizations and how to develop critical, self-reflection that was to influence the work for which he is most recognized, and for his idea of practitioners reflecting-*in*-action – this is the kind of reflection that takes place in real time and as a consequence of emergent challenges or observations on what is happening. Schön (1983, 1987) was convinced that professionals "know" more than they can articulate and was interested in getting them to articulate what they "know" and "do" by engaging in this process of reflection-in-action. As Schön (1983, p. 50) observed, the "know-how is in the action." Thus, he suggested that practitioners become more aware of what they do as they perform by observing their actions, or by reflecting-*in*-action. Schön (1983) suggests that reflection-in-action happens in uncertain, unique situations, when routine action leads to some unexpected results (good or bad). This, of course, all depends on the practitioner's awareness of that "situation."

For language teachers, Freeman (2016) suggests that the "uniqueness is not in the situation, but in how the individual approaches, thinks about, and 'frames' it" (p. 201). The practitioner uses the knowledge obtained during this framing process while "reflecting-in-action . . . thinking what they are doing and, in the process, evolving their way of doing it" (Schön, 1983, p. 56). The result may lead to some modification or adjustment or possibly doing the same again. Schön (1983, p. 62) maintains that the adjustment time frame, or, as he calls it, "'action-present,' the zone of time in which action can still make a difference to the situation," as the practitioner reflects-in-action may "stretch over minutes, hours, days, weeks or even months." Thus, in a Deweyan sense, a temporal pause (where the practitioner attempts to reshape what he or she is doing while he or she is doing it) may be necessary between reflection and action and when making any readjustments to an action. For Schön (1983, p. 18), then, "problem setting," or finding the problem in the first place, is as important as solving it and depends on the level of awareness of each individual practitioner in situations of practice that are unique to the individual practitioner.

Many scholars have credited Schön's work with directing the attention of teacher educators to the concept of reflection in teacher education and development (Freeman, 2016; Loughran, 2002; Rogers, 2002; Zeichner, 1983). One reason for this may have been that Dewey's approach to reflection maintained that the practitioner suspend action when confronted with a problem and after going through his steps of reflective inquiry, to take action only in the final stage, whereas Schön (1983) encouraged the practitioner to continue to reflect during action (or "action present") in an attempt to reshape what the practitioner is doing while he or she is doing it.

I chose to include the subheading "standing on the shoulders of giants" for this section because without these two great scholars' approaches to refection and reflective practice, I would not have any basis to understand this interesting, yet complex concept and I would not have been able to develop my own framework for reflecting on practice. Dewey (1933) is widely acknowledged as the founder of the reflective practice movement in modern times, and he considered reflective practice as intentional, systematic inquiry that was disciplined and that would ultimately lead to change and professional growth for teachers (reflection-*on*-action). Schön built on Dewey's work and added to this the idea of a practitioner being able to reflect on his or her intuitive knowledge while engaged in the action of teaching (or reflection-*in*-action).

The legacy of Dewey and Schön is important because they moved the concept of reflection far beyond everyday simple wonderings about a situation to a more rigorous form of evidence-based thinking where a teacher systematically investigates a perceived "problem" in order to discover a solution. Engaging in evidence-based reflective practice allows teachers to articulate to themselves (and others) what they do, how they do it, why they do it, and what the impact of one's teaching is on student learning. In addition, both Dewey's and Schön's work suggest that teachers can look at what is actual and occurring (theories-in-use) in their practice and compare this to their beliefs (espoused theories) about learning and teaching because, for many, the espoused theories may not work in action and thus the teacher must develop new theory within that action. This *productive tension* (Donald Freeman, personal communication) between "espoused theories" and "theories-in-use" can provide teachers with the opportunity to examine their practice so that they can deepen their understanding of what they do and thus gain new insights about their students, their teaching, and themselves. As Dewey (1933) noted, growth comes from a "reconstruction of experience" (p. 87), and by reflecting on these experiences we can reconstruct our own approaches to teaching. That said, Hébert (2015) cautions against any "uncritical adoption of reflective models, stressing that in doing so, the very spirit of reflective practice can be undermined" (p. 381).

2.1.2 Constraints

I now outline some of the constraints I see in both Dewey's and Schön's work, not to disparage them in any way, but rather to use them to further develop the concept of reflection and reflective practice within the language teaching profession. For example, one constraint is in Dewey's suggestions that reflection must always begin with some type of problem that upsets the routine of daily practice and that needs to be tackled and solved immediately, or, as Dewey (1933) stated, the reflection process begins with "a shock or an interruption needing to be accounted for, identified, or placed" (p. 12). The practitioner then proceeds through the five phases of reflective inquiry with the final goal "that results in the alleviation of doubt by way of certainty, or at least, as close to certainty as possible" (Hébert, 2015, p. 363). However, this excludes situations of practice that do not create doubt, such as a more critical stance toward how use of a particular textbook set within a curriculum reflects the values of the teachers and the students within a community or context. As Ecclestone (1996) also notes, such a technical-rationalist approach to reflection "divorces values from techniques and methods" (p. 148). Thus, Dewey's (1933) reflective inquiry focuses almost exclusively on solving problems but does not encourage any critical reflection beyond immediate practice.

Linked to the constraint associated with reflection that must be initiated by a shock or a problem is Dewey's idea that the problem itself *must* be solved. Thus, Dewey's reflective inquiry approach can be classified as an "ends-based model" (Hébert, 2015, p. 363) that must always begin with a problem and then uncover a solution. This notion that there must be some kind of conclusive (and mostly positive) result to the reflective inquiry process has also seeped into the recent action research movement within language teaching that I outlined in Section 2.1.1, where teachers usually only examine classroom-based problems of practice that need to be corrected. In other words, there is no room for doubt or uncertainty, as problems must be repaired. However, I believe that when language teachers explore, examine, and reflect, for example, on critical incidents that occur frequently within classrooms, they quickly realize how complex and uncertain the teaching process is and, as a result, need to develop a tolerance for ambiguity because there are no simple solutions or answers available. I also include such encouragement of a tolerance for ambiguity in my framework by encouraging language teachers to reflect on critical incidents both inside and outside the classroom.

One more constraint I think is important to note regarding Dewey's approach is that there is some kind of distance between the practitioner and the problem during the reflection process. In fact, it seems that the person who is doing the reflection is standing on the outside looking at the problem. In other words, the teacher is separated from the act of teaching and the "problem" that needs to be "fixed" exists outside the person who is doing the reflection, or the teacher-as-person. Thus, reflection and problem-solving seem to exist outside the person-as-teacher. I return to this issue in Section 2.2.1 when I outline my framework, but for now I maintain that the person-as-teacher cannot be divorced from the act of teaching and reflection, and so I believe that reflection is grounded in the notion that teachers are whole persons and the person-as-teacher should be a part of the reflection process.

Similarly to Dewey's approach of relating reflection nearly exclusively to problem-solving, Schön's experiential-intuitivist model of reflection was criticized for focusing on problem-solving (Hébert, 2015). Although Schön (1983) attempted to address Dewey's technical rationalist temporal gap between reflection and action through his reflection-*in*-action (or "action present," as noted in Section 2.1.1) approach, his model similarly proceeds along a "causal chain" (Hébert, 2015, p. 366) that is also initiated by a problem of some kind that results in the practitioner becoming uncertain. As the practitioner moves along that "chain" and reflects-in-action, he or she ultimately ends up reflecting-*on*-action, like what Dewey proposed. Indeed, as Collin, Karsenti, and Komis, (2013) have argued, "reflection-in-action may therefore be retrospective, which blurs the distinction from reflection-on-action" (p. 109).

Another constraint I suggest connected to Schön's (1983) reflecting on "situations of practice" with learner teachers especially is the difficulty of recognizing individual teachers' unique reflections, which are different from those of the teacher educator overseeing the process of reflection. Within language teaching, as Freeman (2016) has pointed out, although the teacher educators may see different issues, or "situations," in lessons they observe, they "cannot see them on behalf of" the learner teachers they are observing (p. 210). In other words, for some learner teachers, particular "situations" may be taken as "problematic," but not for others. Thus, I believe that when language teachers are asked to reflect on their practices, teacher educators and administrators must consider whose interests are being pursued/met: the teacher educator' or the teacher? As a result, I have frequently proposed that when language teachers reflect through the lens of the framework outlined in this Element, it is used as a kind of mirror for descriptive accounts of what occurs without (prescriptive) critiques from teacher educators or supervisors, or those who are facilitating the reflective process. The main idea of encouraging teachers of all levels to engage in reflective practice is that they take responsibility for their decisions and actions inside and outside their lessons (I address this in more detail in Section 4).

In addition, I think it is important that teacher educators consider that when learner teachers are requested to reflect, often a top-down, "reflect on demand" type of imposed power differential is attached to the process wherein what teacher educators consider to be important "situations" override the perceptions of the learner teacher doing the reflecting. The likely outcome of such reflection is one of compliance, where the teacher looks to the supervisor for "what to reflect on" while going through the motions, or as Hobbs (2007) put it, "faking it or hating it" (p. 405). Thus, teacher educators must be aware of the power dynamics present and be on guard against such top-down imposed reflections in order to allow learner teachers to see their *own situations* of practice.

One further but very important constraint associated with Schön's (1983) approach to reflection outlined by Boud and Walker (1998) is that his analysis ignores critical features of the context of reflection. As Boud and Walker point out, context is "the single most important influence on reflection and learning" (p. 197). They define context as "the total cultural, social and political environment in which reflection takes place" (p. 196). They note that this larger context, although mirrored in local contexts, is also further modified within these settings such as educational settings that include the institution, the classroom, the curriculum, and any other context-specific social and cultural aspects of that setting. Their point is that the context will influence the type and methods of reflection possible. They maintain that, when considering the importance of context in the reflection process, practitioners should consider:

- their awareness of what elements of the cultural, institutional, or disciplinary context may need to be filtered or confronted in this local context, or which may be used to advantage in the learning event (i.e., a particular session in a course);
- how they can cope with the demands of the institution within which they operate; and
- their own power and the ways in which this might impact learners singularly and collectively.

In summary, I value Dewey and Schön's approaches to reflective practice because both took a pragmatic rather than a theoretical approach to reflection and reflective practice. In addition, Dewey emphasized evidence-based, systematic collection of data about practice and then using such evidence to make more informed decisions about practice. I also agree with Schön's additions to reflecting while doing the action, or reflection-*in*-action, in that practitioners should not only reflect after the event. However, I note that both approaches also have constraints or limitations because they are both ends-based models where problems must be solved regardless of when they occur (*in*-action or *on*-action). In other words, there is no room for uncertainty and the practitioner seems somewhat detached from the reflection process. I believe that reflection should not only begin with seeking answers to a problem but also allow for some kind of uncertainty in that we may not reach a clear solution. In addition, values should be interwoven with the reflection process itself. It was with these constraints that I was prompted to develop the more holistic approach to reflective practice for language teachers that is outlined in the next section.

2.2 A Holistic Approach to Reflecting on Practice for Language Teachers

Both Dewey's and Schön's perspectives on reflection and reflective practice have had immense influence on my own work, especially the development of my new framework for reflecting on practice for language teachers (Farrell, 2015). Like Dewey, I consider reflective practice as a form of systematic inquiry that is rigorous and disciplined, and, like Schön, I am interested in how teachers "think on their feet" or how they reflect, not only *in* action and *on* action, but also *for* action. Reflection-*for*-action is different from reflection-in-action and reflection-on-action in that it is proactive in nature. Killion and Todnem (1991) maintain that reflection-*for*-action can be the desired outcome of both previous types of reflection. They point out that "we undertake reflection, not so much to revisit the past or to become aware of the metacognitive process one is experiencing (both noble reasons in themselves) but to guide future action (the more practical purpose)" (p. 15). I have also incorporated reflection-for-action, or anticipatory reflection, in my framework because, as Stanley (1998) has noted, all three are what "reflective practitioners do when they look at their work in the moment (reflect-in-action) or in retrospect (reflect-on-action) in order to examine the reasons and beliefs underlying their actions and generate alternative actions for the future" (p. 585).

Dewey's and Schön's legacies are important because they moved the concept of reflection far beyond everyday simple wonderings about a situation (or mulling over something without taking action) to a more rigorous form of reflective thinking whereby a teacher systematically investigates a perceived problem in order to discover a workable solution over time. I realize that I was attracted to their work because they were very pragmatic in their approaches so that they could help practicing teachers on the front lines. However, I also saw a need to explore other modes, approaches, and typologies beyond the confines (noted in Section 2.1.2) of Dewey's and Schön's approaches. With the idea that reflective practice may not be the same as the practice of reflection, I also reexamined other models and frameworks (some were follow-ups to Dewey's and Schön's works; others were different) to see if these held any useful points for me to consider as I attempted to expand my understanding of reflective practice and the practice of reflection. I outline some of their influences on the development of my own framework in what follows.

Kolb's (1984) approach, for example, is influential in that he focuses on practice and can guide teachers in a systematic way on how to examine the success or otherwise of their lessons and to seek improvement as a result of such reflections. While I agree somewhat with this approach and include many of these elements in my own current framework, Kolb does not take the teacher-as-person into consideration in terms of his or her identity and the impact of social and political elements on such reflections. However, his work was further developed by Gibbs's (1988) reflective cycle to help with the professional development of nursing practitioners, and he included the practitioners' emotions while reflecting. This is a positive addition to the typologies on reflective practice because there is a consideration of the practitioners' feelings while reflecting on a particular experience. I agree with this. However, I would bring it further and include an emotional/affective aspect of reflection beyond just reflecting on a particular event or experience to include critical reflection on all aspects of our work. Thus, I believe we must be on guard against intellectualizing reflection as solely a cognitive process by stepping back too far from the person-as-teacher who is doing the reflection, and instead recognize the emotional, affective aspects of reflection. An important addition to the development of my framework for reflecting on practice includes this crucial aspect of reflecting on emotions associated with practice.

I studied Johns's (1995) model of reflection within the nursing profession and I agree with him that reflection is "a way of being" or a daily occurrence on a personal and professional level. As a result, I believe that reflection is not a one-off event, but a lifelong endeavor for language teachers. That said, I do not believe that language teachers should engage each day in intensive reflections, as this would be too much and would probably have a negative effect on their students' learning. Rather, I believe that teaching experience should be interspersed with periods of reflection throughout a teacher's career so that he or she does not plateau (e.g., see Farrell, 2014). In that manner, and similarly to what Johns has noted, reflective practice can become a way of life for language teachers both professionally and personally within their daily lives.

I also agree with Brookfield's (1995) idea of critical lenses (see also Dewey's reflective inquiry in Section 2.1.1), as these lenses give us more insight into what we as individuals could be unwittingly blocking from our "vision" about what we do. It may not be easy to look at ourselves professionally, and it is very difficult to look at ourselves personally, thus bringing in others to facilitate reflection offers us other views about our practice that we may not be able to "see" if we reflect alone. When we ask colleagues to help us look, we can develop a sense of community, and when we ask our students about our teaching, we are getting them to engage in reflective learning. All this is a win-win outcome for everyone involved in the community.

One final model that has influenced the development of the framework outlined later in this Element is the approach to reflective practice proposed by psychologists Shapiro and Reiff (1993). Their approach focused on addressing the needs of experienced professionals who wished to get a better understanding of their practices. Their model outlined a process of *reflective inquiry on practice* (RIP). Their process of reflection began at level 1 with an examination of *philosophy* of practice, or the person behind the practice. This was followed by level 2 reflections called *basic theory* (they considered this less influential than philosophy because it may be derived from philosophical premises). Level 3 reflections outlined a *theory of practice* that also included what they called *theory of techniques* embedded in a general approach to practice. This was followed by level 4 reflections called *technique* where practitioners reflect on their deliberate professional behavior, including examining their lectures, role-playing, dialogues, panel discussions, group problem-solving activities, simulations, and any other activities they engaged in. Level 5, the final level of reflections, was called *interventions or moves*. They suggested that *moves* are behaviors that are directly observed in professional practice.

Shapiro and Reiff (1993) maintain that their framework is similar in purpose to Argyris and Schön's (1974) reflection and double-loop learning (see Section 2.1.1) through understanding the various relationships between and among the different levels of their model to improve professional practice, and they also note that the reflection should take place in the context of a supportive group situation (and, as Dewey suggested, in collaboration with others). However, what is different from the work of Schön (1983, 1987) is, most notably, that they focus on reflection-*on*-action – that is, after the event – and not *in*-action during the event itself. In addition, their framework was designed exclusively to help experienced professionals (mostly psychologists) and encouraged them to engage in Kolb's (1984) reflective observation so that they could notice patterns in their practice.

2.2.1 The Framework

The framework presented in this Element also consists of five stages similar to Shapiro and Reiff's (1993) framework; however, these stages focus on different aspects of reflection after a similar beginning focus on philosophy and I add the important aspect of critical reflection which I call reflecting *beyond practice* in the framework that includes emotional reflection, achieved through appraisal analysis. In this Element, I have chosen to focus my discussion mainly on Dewey's and Schön's models of reflection, their perspectives, and some of their shortcomings, because they have been so influential on my work on reflective practice over the past forty years. I also attempted to incorporate Gibbs's (1988) reflection on practitioners' emotions, Johns's (1995) consideration of reflection as "a way of being," Brookfield's (1995) idea of critical lenses, and Shapiro and Reiff's (1993) structured approach to developing the framework. In addition, I also studied many other approaches, many of which I conclude overlook the inner lives of teachers. I think this separation of the reflector from what is being reflected on is the result of reflection being reduced to a problem-solving activity where the sole aim is to fix rather than understand the problem. Such a focus on "reflection-as-repair" (Freeman, 2016, p. 217) reduces reflection to more ritualistic and mechanical technical rationality that defeats the original spirit of reflection. When students are asked to reflect on demand by following a sequence of steps outlined in predetermined checklists or a trajectory of set questions, reflection becomes one-dimensional and is confined to a retrospective "post-mortem" (Freeman, 2016, p. 217) role. The result of such approaches to reflection is that teachers have been required for the most part to follow a set of checklists designed by others when reflecting.

Thus, with this framework, I believe that engaging in reflective practice should not result in technical, rational teachers; rather it should result in integrated teachers because they have knowledge of who they are (their *philosophy*), why they do what they do (their *principles*), what they want to do (their *theory*), how they do it (their *practice*), and what it all means to them within their community (beyond *practice*). The framework is outlined in Figure 1.

I now briefly outline each stage.

Philosophy: This first stage maintains, similarly to Shapiro and Reiff's (1993) ideas, that practice, both inside and outside the classroom, is invariably guided by a teacher's basic philosophy, or the "teacher-as-person," and that this philosophy has been developing since birth. Thus, self-knowledge is an essential first step for teachers in working through the framework, but it is often overlooked in earlier literature on reflective practice. Teachers can obtain self-knowledge by exploring, examining, and reflecting on their background – from

Figure 1 Framework for reflecting on practice (Farrell, 2015)

where they have evolved – such as heritage, ethnicity, religion, socioeconomic background, family, and personal values that have combined to influence who they are now as language teachers. Reflecting on their philosophy of practice can not only help teachers flesh out what has shaped them as human beings, and how their past experiences may have shaped the construction and development of their basic philosophy, but it can also help them move onto the next level of reflection, reflecting on their principles.

Principles: The second stage of the framework, principles, includes reflections on teachers' assumptions and beliefs about teaching and learning English as a subsequent language. Teachers' practices and their classroom instructional decisions are often formulated and implemented (for the most part subconsciously) on the basis of their underlying assumptions and beliefs because these are the driving forces (along with philosophy reflected on at stage one) behind many of their classroom actions. Thus, reflecting on principles of teaching and learning enables teachers to uncover their beliefs and gain a deeper awareness of their teaching practice.

Theory: Theory explores and examines the different choices teachers make about particular language skills taught (or they think should be taught) or, in other words, how to put their theories into practice. Influenced by their reflections on their philosophy and principles, teachers actively begin to construct their theory of practice. Theory at this stage means that teachers consider the type of lessons they want to deliver. All language teachers have theories, both "official" theories we learn in teacher education courses and "unofficial" theories we gain with teaching experience. However, not all teachers may be fully aware of these theories, especially their "unofficial" theories that are sometimes called "theories-in-use." Reflections at this stage/level in the framework include considering all aspects of teachers' planning and the different activities and methods teachers choose (or may want to choose) as they attempt to put theory into practice. Teachers can also examine critical incidents, or any unplanned events that happen during a class, outside a class, or during their career, that are "vividly remembered" (Brookfield, 1990, p. 84). When a critical incident occurs, it interrupts (or highlights) the taken-for-granted ways of thinking about teaching and, by analyzing such incidents, language teachers can develop a clearer understanding of theory and practice. Although I include critical incidents in this stage, they can be included and do occur throughout the stages as Playsted (2019) outlined.

Practice: The fourth stage, *practice*, provides an opportunity for language teachers to explore what they do in their classrooms and to closely examine connections between their philosophy, principles, and theory with more visible actions and thus note any "discrepancy between what we do and what we think we do" (Knezevic, 2001, p. 10). At this stage/level in the framework, teachers can reflect while they are teaching a lesson (reflection-*in*-action), after they teach a lesson (reflection-*on*-action), or before they teach a lesson (reflection-*for*-action). Although Schön (1983, p. 56) maintained that reflection-*in*-action does not have to be "in the medium of words" (as when jazz musicians "feel" the music), my framework suggests that the medium of language is probably necessary to describe such reflection because as Freeman (2016, p. 215) has noted, "languaging reflection-on-action" can help teachers explain what they do by creating a separation between "the lived present and a languaged past" (p. 216), thus making the private individual reflections more public. When teachers engage in reflection-*on*-action, they are examining what happened in a lesson after the event has taken place, and this is a more delayed type of reflection as they go through Dewey's (1933) steps in his reflective inquiry model. When teachers engage in reflection-*for*-action, they are attempting to reflect before anything has taken place and to anticipate what may happen and try to account for this before they conduct the lesson.

Beyond practice: The final stage, *beyond practice* or *critical reflection*, explores the moral, political, emotional, ethical, and community/social issues that impact teachers' practices both inside and outside the classroom. Beyond practice here means that language teachers reflect beyond their methods and if they "work" or not to other issues that they must also deal with on a daily basis, such as community and political issues that can impact who they are as teachers and what they do inside and outside their classrooms. Reflections at this stage can assist teachers in becoming more aware of the many political agendas and economic interests that can (and do) shape how we define language teaching and learning. They can become more aware of the impact of their lessons on their community (this also includes the virtual community) and the impact of that community on their practice. At this critical reflection stage, in this Element, I have now added more emphasis on how researchers, teachers, and teacher educators can specifically access, explore, and reflect more precisely on teacher emotions by examining teachers' affective language through the lens of the Appraisal Framework (Martin, 2000; Martin & White, 2005; White, 2000). A central component of the Appraisal Framework is exploration of language for expressing attitude that consists of three subsystems: *affect*, *judgment*, and *appreciation* (White, 2000), with *affect* referring to the language used for expressing emotions. I believe that this will better "emotionalize" (Holmes, 2010) the concept of reflective practice so we can better account for the emotional aspects of professional experiences and for how emotions contribute to the making of and reflections on professional language teaching practices (Brookfield, 1995).

The framework is descriptive rather than prescriptive in that it does not suggest mapping out so-called best practice. As Edwards and Thomas (2010) cautioned, "reflective practice cannot be a prescriptive rubric of skills to be taught [to teachers]; in fact, to see it in this way reverts to the very technicist assumptions reflective practice was meant to exile" (p. 404). Over recent years, I have conducted such evidence-based holistic reflective practice research using the framework in Section 2.2.1 (but without specific reference to the emotional aspects of reflecting on practice that are present in this Element), with the idea that the teachers will benefit as a means of making their own informed decisions about teaching (e.g., Farrell & Kennedy, 2019; Farrell & Macaplinac, 2021).

3 Reflective Practice in Action

In this section, I introduce the most recent in-depth case study that I conducted with an EFL teacher in Costa Rica, in Central America, who used the expanded framework as a lens to reflect on his teaching. I also include how I explored his use of emotive language as he engaged in reflective practice throughout the process.

3.1 Background to the Study

The English language has been a prominent focus in education throughout Central America due to several factors including tourism, economic expansion, proximity to English-speaking countries, and interest in science and biodiversity (Aguilar-Sánchez, 2005). In 2008, the Costa Rican government officially declared English learning "a matter of national interest" (Campos, 2012, p. 169). The government has implemented several policies to establish English as the first foreign language and, as a result, teachers must follow the National Syllabus for English. This syllabus states that English prepares students to face challenges that require an additional language, gain integrated knowledge of the world, and actively engage in the global economy to benefit the country (MEP, 2001). In an effort to make English education more accessible in Central America, local governments opened nonprofit binational schools in most major cities. These schools offer a range of programs for different audiences, all in alliance with the National Geographic Learning Curriculum (Inforcostarica, 2000). Notably, there is a scholarship program for students who are of low socioeconomic status but earned high academic standing after high school. Most teachers are non-native speakers of English, but they must have an academic background in teaching, hold a score of 950 on the Test of English for International Communication (TOEIC), and have at least one year of teaching experience. English as a foreign language teachers are usually contracted to teach up to three classes of three hours in length, every day except Sunday.

The teacher highlighted in the case study reported in this Element teaches EFL to local adult students at a nonprofit binational center for English teaching in Costa Rica. The institution prioritizes speaking skills and knowledge of L2 English grammar. The teacher, Damien (a pseudonym), has been teaching EFL for five years and holds a bachelor's degree in English teaching as a second language (ETSL) from a local university. Damien expressed interest in this study after having completed several research projects during his own post-secondary studies.

The study commenced in 2020 shortly after the global outbreak of the COVID-19 pandemic when Damien had hitherto been teaching in traditional classrooms. Upon receiving news of government-mandated school closures, Damien transitioned all instruction to synchronous online learning beginning in March 2020. Students in existing classes were expected to participate in virtual classes from their home computers using a video conference platform for the remainder of the academic term. In addition to school closures, nonessential businesses in many countries suspended operations or exercised restrictions and directed employees to work from home. Damien moved to using the online platform Zoom from his home.

Data collection took place over one month and included semi-structured interviews and follow-up interviews that were subsequently transcribed, written reflection tasks, and virtual classroom observations in line with Farrell's (2015) reflective framework.[2] Responses were sought to a main research question – what are Damien's reflections as expressed through his philosophy, principles, theory, practice, and beyond practice? Six interviews were conducted: one preinterview to clarify basic information and five follow-up interviews

---

[2] My thanks to Connie Stanclik for help with data collection and initial interpretation of data

following each stage of the reflective practice framework. All interviews were conducted and recorded via Zoom and lasted between thirty and forty-five minutes (Maxwell, 1992). In addition, three different classes per week were observed and recorded on Zoom and each class was later transcribed. Damien also completed six written reflection tasks (by e-mail) that explored his philosophy, principles, theory, practice, and beyond practice, and these were later used as springboards for questions in follow-up interviews.

Data were coded using a priori theory to structure initial levels of the coding scheme and later organized into different categories according to the stage of framework for reflective practice, which was, "open, axial, and selective" (Merriam, 2009, p. 200). In order to make sense of the data, recurring patterns were then grouped and compared against the research question. In addition, for each observed lesson, I had access to Damien's lesson plan to help analyze the objectives and compare his intentions with what he actually delivered during the lesson. Member checking was used as a means of confirming the validity of the data (Lincoln & Guba, 1985). I shared Damien's complete descriptive reflections (i.e., the findings outlined in Section 3.2) with him so that he could reflect on these descriptions without any comments, analysis, or interpretations. I believe that teachers constructing their own meaning, understanding, and knowledge of their practice is more important than creating a condition of what Fanselow (1988) has called "learned helplessness" (p. 145), when others provide the analysis. Fanselow notes that providing "help" can not only lead to resentment but can also stop the exploration of teaching that reflective practice is designed to encourage. As Fanselow (1988) explains, "helpful prescriptions can stop exploration, since the receiver, as someone in an inferior position being given orders by someone in a superior position, may easily develop the 'ours is not to wonder why' syndrome" (p. 114).

3.2 Findings (Damien's Reflections)

The findings are presented as answers to the main research question: what are Damien's reflections as expressed through his philosophy, principles, theory, practice, and beyond practice?

3.2.1 Philosophy

Damien said his family members have been influential in his life, specifically when they encouraged him to pursue teaching because, in his view, they believed he possessed the necessary traits to succeed in the field. He shared that, during his teacher education program, he had had positive experiences. He also noted that he was involved in conducting multiple research projects and that, as a result, he was excited when he heard about this opportunity to participate in a reflective practice study. Damien viewed his participation in this study, and specifically the concept of reflective practice, as a new skill for him to learn.

Reflecting on the self, Damien described himself as a good listener. He believes that he has always possessed this trait and that it comes from a desire to help and learn from others. He expressed that meeting new people since becoming a teacher has exposed him to new experiences and expanded his natural sense of curiosity. He said that throughout his career, he hopes "to learn about all things" that will help him develop his practice. Damien recounted that some of his prior jobs in the service industry solidified his desire to help others and he had established high ethical standards for himself as a professional.

Related to setting high ethical standards for himself, Damien also maintained that he has a perfectionist attitude and therefore often found himself frustrated when he began teaching. However, he did not elaborate on what aspects of teaching frustrated him at this time of the project other than noting that teachers should not be totally responsible for providing positive learning opportunities and that institutions also have such a responsibility. He did nonetheless elaborate in the post-project interview about current frustrations related to his teaching situation that would eventually lead him to stop teaching at this institute after the project ended. I discuss this in more detail later in this section.

3.2.2 Principles

Regarding language learning, Damien remarked that he believes such learning should occur in a friendly and positive environment where students are encouraged to express themselves freely. He relayed that giving students opportunities to express their opinions and interests helps them learn "just to be able to communicate in the language" without fear of making mistakes. He believes learning should be fun, and he enjoys sharing activities and information students may find interesting in their free time, such as pop culture content or news articles related to topics discussed in class. Damien noted that this principle has been helpful for him in the transition to online learning, as the new medium has impacted the atmosphere of his classroom:

> Before online classes, it was super easy and everything in the classroom was a very nice atmosphere. The last bi-mester was the first one we started teaching online. I had a couple of complications also with a couple of students. Nothing too serious, nothing that I would stress over a lot. This bi-mester, I thought it was going to be easier, and it was in some ways, but the type of students made it a little difficult.

Next, Damien talked about language teaching and that he believes that teaching through what he called "communicative learning" gives him more flexibility to gauge his students' needs. Damien also noted the importance of balancing his students' needs with job expectations. While he noted that his institution sets clear guidelines and learning goals, Damien believes that "not everyone learns the same way, especially in the type of classes we have." This motivates him to consider the needs of different students. Furthermore, he reported that "most important, the people [who] come to our place are also from companies and so they need English for different purposes." Thus, he remarked, it is important for him to be aware of these purposes in order to tailor his practice to specific needs and goals as they emerge. "I have different ways to present the information to students, so it is understandable, and everyone [somehow] gets the idea at the end." This articulates his belief about the efficacy of communicative learning while simultaneously revealing a degree of uncertainty because the curriculum does not always accommodate this. Admittedly, he said that he cannot always address every student's specific needs, but he believes that being flexible and adaptive is the key to navigating needs as they are encountered. Damien also noted that he believes building rapport with students is an important aspect of language teaching. He admitted that it was challenging to connect with students during his first year of teaching but that now, five years on, he views connnec-tion as a tool for gaining a greater understanding of how best to deliver his lessons.

Because the institution Damien works in prioritizes speaking skills, Damien talked about his beliefs related to teaching this skill. However, he also said that he believes that his students should also have a good knowledge of L2 English grammar, noting that he continues to include this in his teaching. Regarding the teaching of L2 speaking, Damien said that teaching L2 speaking should enable learners to use the language in meaningful ways because the students in his class "need the language for something, irrespective of individual purposes." He explained that this requires him to learn more about his students' learning styles and purposes for attending class, which can vary greatly depending on the size of the class. He also noted that, while teaching L2 speaking he has an important role in managing interaction, he said:

> There is as much chance for interaction as the teacher allows it. I feel like I have a lot of control over (and maybe can monitor better) the time I allow for interaction. However, this is something that has to be well designed beforehand.

Damien believes that managing interaction should be a curated step in the lesson-planning process, especially in online classrooms. He said teachers are responsible for creating an environment where student-to-student interaction is plentiful and expressed that he is always trying to encourage more of it in the midst of online learning.

Damien further noted that while teaching L2 speaking, using L1 to facilitate comprehension for low-level learners is important. Although his institution employs an "English only" policy, Damien maintained that incorporating some L1 is necessary when accommodating low-level students struggling with comprehension and output. He recalled that "there are a couple of students who are having a hard time and I cannot just leave them behind." Moreover, he justified that utilizing L1 at times is the most realistic and practical approach to addressing immediate needs and that pushing students beyond their current capabilities may have negative repercussions:

> I was having a hard time having them speak English. So that was my only concern this bi-mester (term), that a lot of them would fail and I guess they're going to fail, unfortunately. But it's for the best because if they go to another level when they are not prepared, it's going to be more difficult for them and for the next teacher too.

Regarding L2 grammar, Damien expressed that students' understanding basic grammar rules is essential for good L2 proficiency. When asked about how knowledge of grammar builds linguistic competence, he remarked, "there are some patterns that we need to recognize to learn a language, but the way every individual manages to recognize these patterns varies." While overall Damien follows a communicative approach to his teaching, he also believes that L2 grammar has an important role in creating a framework for language learning, which he acknowledged is "recognized and interpreted differently among learners." Damien also contended that recognizing grammar patterns and practicing language are important. He recounted that making time to practice new grammar concepts is something he always aims to incorporate in his teaching. Since transitioning to online learning, Damien assigns certain grammar activities for homework that would have previously been completed during class. He said that he does this to "take advantage of (class) time for practice and for speaking, because sometimes reviewing this grammar takes a lot of time from the class." By teaching this way, he is still adhering to institution guidelines for using class time to focus on speaking skills. Damien ensures his students receive adequate opportunities to learn and practice language patterns in order to deepen their understanding of L2 grammar.

Damien's beliefs are primarily grounded in his experience of what works best in the classroom and his institution's established practices (Richards & Lockhart, 1994). He recounted that his daily work experiences and the experiences of his colleagues impact his teaching beliefs but ultimately he chooses to uphold established practices while maintaining some of his own beliefs. "At the end of the day, I teach based on the expectations from my workplace because we have to comply with certain standards, but I try to make space for my own beliefs." Using his experiences to make decisions and adhering to his institution's expectations reinforces his recurrent belief that flexibility is an important attribute of a successful teacher.

3.2.3 Theory

Damien reflected on his lesson-planning and delivery procedures in his classroom and said that his primary concerns when planning are trying to achieve all the goals and outcomes emphasized at his institution and assessments, which he admitted rarely happens. Damien tries to engage in "forward planning," where lesson content has precedence over teaching methods and activities. In other words, the teacher begins by identifying the content to be taught and only then decides activities and methods to be used to achieve this plan, which is assessed at the end of the lesson. Such planning is generally used at institutions with mandated curricula and textbooks and centrally designed assessments (Richards, 2013). Damien mentioned that he takes a more general approach to planning now that his institution does not require teachers to submit a detailed lesson plan for each class as it did in the past. Although he has had opportunities to teach many courses over his five-year career at the institution, Damien relayed that he continues to revise his planning procedures.

> If it's a level that I haven't taught in a while, then I just try to maybe read what I planned for those classes and if I have some new ideas, I definitely get rid of the old ones and try to implement ideas that would work better now in this context for students. And so that's basically what I do.

Reviewing his past work serves as a reminder of what works well and what requires adjustment. Due to the COVID-19 pandemic, planning for online classes has taken a new form. Damien explained that planning fewer, meaningful activities via online learning has been more effective than attempting to do the same number of activities that were done in the traditional classroom.

Damien reported that he has approached critical incidents with various solutions and believes that they are opportunities "to set the mood and be a beacon of what we want to achieve every term." In his experience, reducing the use of L1 in the classroom has presented various challenges and incidents (which he did not elaborate on) at different proficiency levels, leading to moments that have shaped his outlook on the issue (see principles in Section 3.2.2 for comments on use of L1 in his classroom). After evaluating and experimenting with competing advice from colleagues, Damien concludes that teachers must know their students best and should use what will motivate their particular students to resolve difficulties.

3.2.4 Practice

For the practice stage of reflection, three lessons of three hours each in length were observed. All lessons, topics, vocabulary, and grammar structures are predetermined on a course syllabus given by the institution. The teacher is required to cover the syllabus but has the freedom to design activities to present the material. Table 1 summarizes Damien's observed practices (on Zoom).

As indicated in Table 1, Damien did not always follow his lesson plans and diverged in two of his observed classes. He explained in the post-observation interviews that his divergence was because of timing issues related to delivering online lessons that he was still dealing with; however, he ensures all necessary material is covered, even if it means "extra work for next time," resulting in the pace of instruction being altered. He noted that "as long as my students learn" was the most important goal; he does not view deviations from his original lesson plan as a negative thing. He explained that timing has been severely impacted by the transfer to online learning because of COVID. "Time goes by a little faster in online platforms if we are not well aware of it." He also reported spending considerably more time on giving and clarifying instructions in oral, visual, and written forms within the online platform. However, one other observed notable deviation from the original lesson plan was in his second lesson when he intentionally cut one activity to spend more time than he initially planned to review a grammar concept from the previous class. When asked about this choice in the post-lesson interview, Damien said that he remembered that a couple of students were absent from the lesson when he introduced the grammar concept and that he wanted them to review it and have the opportunity to address any problems. Despite this deviation, Damien's lessons seemed to achieve his intended goals by maintaining focus on the outcomes while adjusting to unanticipated needs.

Damien was also observed giving feedback and correcting oral errors throughout, as well as incorporating his students' cultural background into the activities. He made use of small group interactions, ensured the students remained on task as much as possible, and remained engaged in informal interactions with his students. He gave students opportunities to speak, either by asking for volunteers or by eliciting responses, followed by any necessary

Table 1 Damien's Observed Practices

Observed Practices	Lesson 1	Lesson 2	Lesson 3
Follow lesson plans	N	N	O
Provide feedback	O	O	O
Correct oral errors	O	O	O
Incorporate students' cultural and/or background knowledge into activities	O	O	O
Be available to students	O	O	O
Engage in informal interactions with students	N	O	N
Keep on task	O	O	O
Perform small group activities	O	O	O
Address individual learners needs/ questions	O	O	O
Allow L1	O	O	O
Teacher Question Types			
Total number of questions asked	90	80	141
Display questions	27	27	66
Referential questions	33	25	41
Questions checking comprehension	19	18	20
Use of "Okay/Right?"	5	6	5
Rephrased/Reformulated questions	2	0	1
Other questions (e.g., informal conversation)	4	4	8
Elicitations			
Total number of elicitations	82	76	121
Correction/Recasts (Oral)	23	12	41
Positive feedback	21	7	21

Note: O: Observed; N: Not observed

corrections and positive feedback, and he allowed his students to use their L1 when answering (Turns 7 to 14 in what follows) without any punishment, as exemplified in the following excerpt from the first observation:

Excerpt 1

1. **St**: Influenza, or flu, is caused by a virus. So "seein" . . . how do you pronounce?
2. **T**: You can pronounce "scientists."
3. **St**: Scientists have to make a new vaccine every year.

4. **T**: Okay, very good, excellent. So here it says that "influenza, or the flu." Remember I told you flu is short for influenza. And can you guys pronounce it "cost"?
5. **Ss**: Cost.
6. **T**: Similar to when you are talking like about the price. I'm going to write it here.
7. **St**: [Using L1], teacher?
8. **T**: What is the meaning?
9. **St**: [Using L1]
10. **T**: Yes, but, [L1]. What is the meaning for?
11. **St**: Cost.
12. **T**: [Using L1]. Remember, what is the meaning for?
13. **St**: What is the meaning for cost?
14. **T**: It means [using L1].

Note: T: teacher; Ss: multiple students; St: specific student

Students were also observed working in small groups using a feature of the video conference platform that creates smaller sessions within the main conference call. This provided opportunities for increased interaction with each other and with the teacher at a lower student-to-teacher ratio. Although Damien believes that students would have more interaction in a traditional classroom, he utilizes this feature to his advantage when implementing discussion activities, which he said have been "less successful" in the online classroom. While students worked in small groups, Damien moved from one session to another to keep students on task and to evaluate the efficacy of the activities.

Related to timing issues, Damien repeatedly remarked that time management is a recurrent issue and that online learning requires a more practical approach. He noted that focusing on simpler activities to achieve learning goals is a better use of his students' time, rather than trying to accomplish the same activities he once planned for traditional classroom delivery. Damien is certain that his students are comfortable informing him if they do not understand instruction, feedback, or new concepts, even with the additional obstacles of online learning. Evidence of this is found is his extensive use of questions and elicitations (although it should be pointed out that many times there was overlap between all question types in each lesson), also summarized in Table 1. Damien asked mostly display questions (39 percent of all questions) to address comprehension and incorporated referential questions (32 percent) and comprehension-checking questions (24 percent) that kept students engaged and promoted the high degree of interaction observed in all three lessons. His preference for prompting more student talk was most notably demonstrated through frequent elicitations during the third lesson (121 elicitations). The following excerpt provides an example:

Excerpt 2

T: All right. Can you also pronounce here "quiet"?

Ss: Quiet.

T: Very good. Number 4. Who can read four?

St: Yes?

T: Who's going to read 4?

St: How does Derek Sieber say people feel when they share their life plan?

T: Mhm. How do people feel when they say, when they share their life plan? Can you pronounce "share"?

Ss: Share.

T: Good. So, the first one says frightened. Can you pronounce "frightened"?

Ss: Frightened.

St: What is the meaning of frightened?

T: Frightened is like scared. Do you know scared?

Ss: Yes.

T: Yeah, like [using L1].

Ss: Frightened.

T: Frightened. I'm going to write the pronunciation. Frightened. The second one, you pronounce it "cheerful."

Ss: Cheerful.

Ss: [Using L1].

T: Yes, similar to happy, that's correct. Cheerful.

St: Cheerful.

T: And what is the last one?

St: Easy, B.

St: Sad.

Ss: [Using L1].

T: Yeah, if you want to say that, you say "tired."

Ss: Tired.

T: You write it like this and you pronounce it like this: "tired."

Ss: Tired.

T: No, not tie-red. Tired.

Ss: Tired.

Note: T: teacher; Ss: multiple students; St: specific student

Furthermore, Damien was observed using Lesson 3 to complete the tasks he did not accomplish in the first two lessons due to the time constraints he mentioned. Although making up for lost time resulted in little informal interaction with students, the significant number of display questions (sixty-six instances) he used in this lesson is probably an indication that he wanted to check for his students' understanding, but it is also noted that he used referential questions (forty-one instances) in this lesson in order to encourage interaction in meaningful ways rather than just checking their comprehension.

3.2.5 Beyond Practice

Damien noted in his critical reflections beyond practice that language education institutions should uphold high ethical standards to ensure that students' language learning experiences are not exclusively the responsibility of the teachers. I am not sure what Damien was referring to regarding his use of "ethical standards" and the role of the institution in which he worked, but he seemed to be struggling with the commercial aspects of language education and his sense of personal responsibility to provide a meaningful educational experience for his students. Damien suggested in one of the interviews that both the school and the teachers should share this responsibility and create a positive learning environment that yields success for the students. Although asked to elaborate, he did not give any further details of what he was thinking. Specifically related to language schools, Damien remarked that while he understands their need to get new students, he was conflicted between the business side of making money and providing a good experience for students learning English. He said that he had experienced this before in his previous career, where marketing systems in place promised more than they could deliver to the customer, and now he is worried about how institutions advertise as a business and less as an educational institution. "We still have to give them good service and give them some benefit, at least the benefit of knowledge."

While suggesting that he is in a challenging profession, Damien said that he appreciates the growth and learning he has experienced since entering the teaching profession (but did not give specific examples) and, as a result, no longer underestimates the influence teachers have on their students and, as an extension, on society as well. This has helped him take responsibility for his role as an impartial judge in the classroom. He described his relationship with students as "friendly and inviting" and acts "as impartial[ly] as possible in every aspect" to ensure any personal bias does not influence learning decisions. He explained that certain reflection-in-action choices must be made in response to students' reactions and that his beliefs about teaching and learning should not interfere with their immediate needs. Notably, Damien's role as a motivator has undergone some changes with the adoption of online learning and limited face-to-face interaction.

> I truly believe that it is necessary to know our student audience and reflect on our teaching practices. I also believe that our role as a teacher is to be a facilitator of knowledge, and so we need to find the best way to transmit this to students.

When asked about how he manages new challenges, he stated that he realizes some issues are "totally out of [his] control," such as students refusing to interact and participate in the virtual classroom. He maintains that the onset of new learning standards does not change his role as a motivator and that, similarly to his early teaching experiences, patience and experience have made it possible to build rapport in the presence of obstacles.

As mentioned in the "beyond practice" explanation of the framework (Section 2.2.1), I have recently added how researchers, teachers, and teacher educators can (and should) examine the emotional aspects of reflective practice. I therefore wondered about Damien's use of emotive language while he was reflecting on his teaching. I outline this aspect of his reflections in this beyond practice stage. I focus the analysis on affect because emotions are usually experienced in the context of affect. Affect is defined as "a feeling encompassing a variety of moods and emotional states that help form the emotional makeup of an individual" (Robbins, Judge, & Campbell, 2017, p. 261). I analyzed all Damien's reflections at each stage for affective language using White's (2000) approach, which include examining the data for *adverbials*: "happily," "angrily," "fearfully," "proudly"; *attributes*: "I'm sad." "He's frightened of spiders"; *nominals*: "His fear was obvious to all"; and *verbs*: "This pleases me." "I hate chocolate." Thus, by applying the categories of affect to the linguistic expressions that appeared in Damien's reflections, I was able to take a deeper look into his use of affective language.

For the most part the results indicate that many of the attitudes Damien expressed as affect were negative expressions. In the philosophy stage, for example, when he was talking about himself as a teacher or person-as-teacher, he said he was *frustrated* (coded attributes) as in the following sentence: "I try to be perfectionist and often get *frustrated* when things don't go as expected when students are learning the language." He also talked about how he had to follow course objectives and how this conflicted sometimes with more practical goals. "Let me see how I can put this. . . . Of course we *need* to follow . . . the goals that each unit of the book has, but I don't know." Need (to follow) was coded as a verb in this instance. Related to the topic of having to follow the curriculum, other words were coded as an attribute such as the word *expected* when he said: "It's [curriculum] something that we are *expected* to follow every time. It's like part of the planning steps that we have. So we should always follow . . . that model." He also used the attribute *unfair* when he was reflecting on his lack of opportunity to advance within the institution because of the system it uses when considering promotion of teachers. "To get a promotion [is] based on . . . our scores and surveys and everything. And sometimes I think it's *unfair* that it's all on us." More negative attributes such as *boring* and *tiring* were used by Damien too when considering his present position as a teacher.

In addition, when he reflected on the clash between his personal ethics and those of the institution in which he worked, he used the attributes *angry* and *offended* as in the following sentence: "I've actually been kind of *angry* at the type of advertising they've been doing for online courses lately. I mean, at least me as a person . . . as an outsider coming to the institution and seeing this, I would feel like kind of *offended* to be honest." In the beyond practice stage too, which focused on his critical reflections of his working conditions, he expressed most dissatisfaction with the extra work he had to do as a result of COVID such as his use of *a lot* (coded as attribute) in the sentence: "Before we would address things there in the moment, but now there's *a lot* of forms to fill out, emails to read and respond." Damien also used an attribute to call the pandemic *heavy* as in the following sentence: "I think that it's [the pandemic] *heavy* on the mind I would say because it's like a recurring thought."

That said, when Damien talked about his students, he expressed more positive language attributes and he showed how much he wanted them to have a good experience with him as their teacher as well as to learn the language. For example, he reflected (perhaps having made his decision to leave the school at this point?), "When I leave this school, my students and colleagues will remember me for being a good friend, [for] always being *receptive*, and for *caring* about them." He also used more positive verbs when he said, "It's because you *want* them to really be competent in the language" and "I'm actually *happy* that at least some of them are and they tell me in class, 'Oh, teacher, I just completed this exercise and this and this and this really helped, or it helped me understand the topic better.'" This analysis of Damien's affective language indicates that when he talked about and reflected on the institution, he used more negative attributes such as "angry," "unfair," and/or "boring," but when he talked about and reflected on his students, he used more positive affective language such as "receptive," "caring," and/or "fun." I return to this aspect of the reflective process in the section that follows.

3.3 Discussion

The foregoing sections outlined Damien's journey through all five stages of the framework for reflecting on practice. Themes that emerged in the findings detail the interconnections and recurring patterns as expressed through his philosophy, principles, theory, practice, and critical reflection. The section then outlines and discusses prominent themes that emerged in Damien's reflections.

A common theme that occurred across all five stages of the framework is the importance of building rapport with students. Indeed, this was evident beginning in his reflection on philosophy and throughout subsequent stages, when he reported that interaction with students and colleagues is the best part of his job. After being raised in a family that he described as "strict," Damien learned through his teaching job that he genuinely enjoys meeting new people and learning from them. His interpersonal tendencies transferred to his principles, as evident in his frequent references to valuing students' purposes for learning and taking time to inquire about this to ensure he provides a positive learning experience. Damien's theory divulged challenges to building rapport, specifically in the context of online learning. Unlike his approach to traditional classroom teaching, Damien reported that he has recently been incorporating humor in his virtual classes to build rapport and increase both student–student interaction and teacher–student interaction. Since beginning online teaching, Damien's planning procedures have remained focused on learning goals and outcomes with the additional dimension of striving to increase interaction. In practice, Damien was observed building rapport with students through informal interactions and frequent use of referential questions. Additionally, he articulated positive feedback and acknowledged students' efforts in various tasks.

Another theme that occurred across all five stages of Damien's reflections was his continued referencing to teaching to students' needs. Damien stated that it is his responsibility to deliver a positive learning experience wherein his students learn successfully. His desire to help others, as discussed in his philosophy, began in childhood and continues to shape his practice. This has shaped his belief that every student has unique needs and experiences that play a part in the language classroom, presenting him with the task of balancing their needs with curriculum expectations. These philosophies and principles align with Damien's theories of adapting lesson plans to suit the needs of his respective students. To learn about his students' needs, Damien asked about their goals and intentions during the first week of classes. In practice, Damien used L1 on multiple occasions to provide adequate and simple explanations to low-level students, followed by a repetition in L2. In doing so, he demonstrated his commitment to making decisions based on students' needs rather than on institutional expectations.

Balancing job expectations and students' needs frequently emerged as a concern when Damien described his practice, notably because he identified issues with regard to the rapid pace of courses. For teachers, the relational and indeed emotional investment involved in teaching includes constant monitoring and listening (and sometimes eliciting) to how their students are feeling and evaluating if they need assistance with their learning; as Isenbarger and Zembylas (2006, p. 123) have observed, "taking the time to listen to students' problems or worries, giving advice or guidance to them." During the third lesson observation, Damien did not diverge from his lesson plan and finished activities that were left incomplete from the previous classes. His students achieved the target learning goals for the lesson, but he did not have time to engage in informal interaction with students the same way he did in the previous classes. Overall, Damien's philosophies, principles, and theories about teaching to students' needs were actualized in his practice and further developed in critical reflection.

Damien reflected on his role as a teacher as being one who finds appropriate strategies to transmit knowledge so that others understand. Damien's journey through the five stages of the framework revealed a primarily cohesive narrative as indicated in his philosophy, principles, theory, and critical reflection and as executed in his classroom practices. Although Damien diverged somewhat from prepared lesson plans in two classes, this may be attributed to issues of time management, although his tendency to address each inquiry in detail was likely another contributing factor. Damien did not interpret this as a bad thing, stating, "they're all very interested in learning and I appreciate that as well because they like to joke and make fun, but they are also committed to learning." Indirectly, his attention to individual students embodies the theme of building rapport. Through critical reflection, Damien reiterated that it is integral for teachers to know and understand their students to be effective educators. Damien's desire to build rapport is demonstrated in his practice behaviors and through consistent allusion throughout his philosophy, principles, theory, and critical reflection. In addition, he critically reflected on the ethics of teaching in an industry motivated by money and his personal ethics of always striving to provide a good learning experience for his students.

Damien's reflection demonstrates the complex nature of beliefs held by teachers that are sometimes in opposition of one another. Farrell and Tan (2008) explored such complex beliefs, reporting that "beliefs exert different degrees of power and influence on the teacher's final classroom practices" (p. 369). For example, the theme of teaching to students' needs remained prevalent as one of Damien's personal beliefs but conflicted with his tendency for adherence to job expectations and curriculum guidelines. While his institution employs an "English only policy," Damien maintains, students struggle at low levels and he does not intend to "leave them behind" by eliminating all L1 in the classroom. Again, his principles conflict with the established practices at his institution, but in this case, he prioritizes students' needs ahead of expectations. Notably, Damien used every instance of student-initiated L1 to model the L2 form, which exemplified both his desire to build rapport and his preference for teaching to students' needs. These clashes between Damien's underlying principles and institutional practices also appeared in the post-project interviews when he noted his institution's tendency to blame its teachers if the students express any negativities rather than taking responsibility itself. He gave as an example "delivering books on time to classes," which is not teachers' fault. Indeed, and as Colnerud (2015) has noted, sometimes the stipulated procedures and practices set by institutions in which teachers work present constraints that make it difficult for teachers like Damien to act in ways that are consistent with their morals.

Garton and Richards (2008) have noted that "the way teachers talk about their experiences is fundamental to understanding how a teacher's knowledge influences what happens in the context of their work" (xxii). Thus, I used the Appraisal Framework to explore Damien's affective language throughout the period of reflection, and results of this extra focus indicate that he tended to use "strong" emotions when expressing some of his ethical dilemmas. This finding seems to have become even more important for the study as I learned indirectly that shortly after taking part in this reflection project, Damien resigned from the institution, and I also learned that he has taken a break from teaching altogether. The analysis of the affective language he used seems to indicate that perhaps he was already heading in such a direction given the mostly recurring strong (and mostly negative) emotions he expressed in many instances as he reflected on his teacher self through his interactions within his intuitional context. As Teng (2017) has noted, "strong emotions may motivate a teacher to take actions that he or she would not normally perform" (p. 118). However, I did not have any further contact with Damien beyond the member checks I did with him when I presented the findings outlined in this Element for his comments; he did not comment on his use of language at that time or on his intentions to leave the institute or teaching altogether.

Teachers as emotional beings are moved by aspects of their work because they are passionate about their practice, and Damien expressed his passion for teaching throughout his reflections. Within the field of language teaching (and with much of the research on reflective practice), however, this (emotional) reality of teaching has not been acknowledged much, and in some instances, it has even been devalued by some administrators who consider the work of English language teaching as only teaching language. Damien has also indicated that this aspect of his contribution had not been recognized or valued at the managerial and administration level at his institution. Indeed, emotions are often at the "epicenter" or heart of teaching (Agudo, 2019; Hargreaves, 2000),

yet language teaching professional and managerial discourse has often neg-
lected this aspect of teachers' well-being in terms of their personal and emotional investment in their practice. Good teachers are not well-oiled machines,
and good teaching is not just a matter of knowing the subject matter or being
able to use all the latest techniques while teaching, or even being efficient. Good
teaching is an emotionally charged event where teachers connect with each
student as they passionately deliver their lesson in a pleasurable environment
(Farrell, 2019b).

Perhaps the research on teaching reflection should move toward a greater
understanding of the teacher self and how teachers' emotions can become sites
of resistance and even self-transformation, both of which may be evident in the
data related to Damien's search for self-knowledge through the lens of reflective
practice. Although both Dewey and Schön acknowledged the place of emotions
in reflective practice, they did not implement any aspects of reflective practice
linked to teacher emotions, and indeed, since its reemergence in the field of
education, reflective practice research has focused on reflection as a cognitive
act that responds to routine teaching "problems" where the teacher as an
emotional being is separated from the act of teaching. Because emotions are
"core" (Holmes, 2010, p. 147) to reflective practice in the context of teaching
practice, Hargreaves (2000) maintains, "cognitive reflection can help us guide
and moderate our emotions and sometimes even wilfully move us into another
emotional state by deciding to brood or cheer ourselves" (p. 412).

Thus, as Teng (2017) reminds us, because "emotions are part of the very
fabric that constitutes the teacher's self" (p. 118), it is important to include the
emotional arena within the realm of reflective practice, especially as we critically reflect on the context of our practice as occurred within Damien's (emotional) reflections outlined in Section 3.2.5. Reflective practice in language
teaching research and practice can add this layer of emotionalizing reflection
as a theoretical and practical tool and generate more empirical explorations and
articulations of emotion dynamics of reflective practice as an integral part of
encouraging language teachers to reflect. However, because emotions are not
only located within the individual who is reflecting, but also are embedded in
and expressed through affective discourse in human interactions and relationships within institutions, we need further research on how language teachers
feel about the emotional aspect of teaching within a particular context or
institution, and how they feel about the various relationships within that context
that teachers have with their students, peers, and administrators. I believe that
the use of the Appraisal analysis and, specifically, a focus on affect (I have
included it in stage 5, "beyond practice") can provide another resource for
enhancing the effectiveness of reflective practice for the development of

language teachers. When language teachers are encouraged to reflect on their philosophy, principles, theory, and practice and to critically reflect beyond practice to include emotional responses at all five stages, this, as Harrison and Lee (2011) point out, shifts the notion of reflective practice from the psychological processes of an individual towards questions that are both moral and technical in nature ... and highlights critical reflective practices as social [and emotional] acts of empowerment" (p. 201).

4 Moving Forward with Reflective Practice: Possibilities for Further Dialogue

The final section concludes the Element by considering how we can move forward with reflective practice in language teaching. Over the years, some scholars in language teaching have wondered if engaging in reflective practice will improve the overall quality of teaching, and if reflection will result in better teaching performance (Akbari, 2007; Borg, 2011). These are very important questions to ask but even more difficult to answer because, when one says "improve quality" or "better performance" for teaching, there is an assumption somewhere that there is some agreed-upon standard out there that is noticeable and measurable and that achieving it will ensure "quality" teaching of some kind.

As mentioned in Section 3.1, I shared the findings of each stage with Damien for his reflections and comments back if he so desired. Damien made the following brief comments after reading each stage: "it was useful to me to reflect on each of the stages as it helps me become more aware and selective of what I do in the class every day." The main point of conducting such evidence-based reflective practice research is to encourage language teachers at all stages of their careers to engage in reflection so that the *teacher* will benefit from it. As Damien noted, "it is great to see all the pieces together as part of a big jigsaw puzzle." Engaging in reflective practice will generate awareness of what a teacher is doing, and as a result of this awareness teachers can make informed decisions about what they would like to "improve" based on that evidence. Again, as Damien observed after reading these findings, he needs to be "more observant and keep a visible track of what I am doing in order to outdo myself every time and not end up doing the same over and over but being more malleable into the best of daily practices."

Some years ago, Argyris and Schön (1974) maintained that the overall purpose of reflection is for the creation of a world that more faithfully reflects its beliefs and values. So engaging in reflective practice allows accountability based on evidence for all stakeholders involved but, most importantly, it gives voice to individual teachers who may have been silenced along the way in their own professional development trajectory. As Damien reflected on his reflections (Section 3.2), he noted, "I feel it is a good thing to take the time to stop and reflect on our teaching practices every now and then." After such reflections on practice, language teachers can consider what they want to align more within their own principles and practices, and thus become generators of practical knowledge, adding to the incomplete knowledge base of language teaching. In addition, and as noted in the previous section, teaching is an emotional act where teachers' emotional experiences can be opportunities to articulate emotions, but such emotional awareness can also help them consider which positive emotions they value and which negative emotions they wish to avoid. Indeed, research has noted that it is more difficult for teachers to reduce negative emotions (such as anger and stress) than to convey positive emotions (such as joy and enthusiasm) when working with students (Freznel et al., 2016). By engaging in reflective practice, language teachers can develop such emotional awareness, and this can assist them to generate more positive emotions so that they can minimize stress and enhance their well-being.

It is possible that Damien's reflective journey through the lens of the framework presented in this Element may have led him to ultimately leave the institution where he was teaching; however, I am not able to verify this assumption. I wonder what may have transpired if I as a facilitator had engaged more with Damien throughout the reflective process about his emotions (both positive and negative) and helped him to develop more "emotional flexibility" (Mackenzie, 2002, p. 186), which could have had a different result than his decision to leave the institution (and ultimately teaching as I discovered later). On the other hand, an alternative interpretation could be that Damien decided to end his employment in the institution because he found that engaging in reflective practice was an emancipating experience for him and, as a result, he decided he wanted to leave.

All through the five stages of the framework, it seems that Damien faced struggles to negotiate dissonance between his personal ethics and his perceptions of the institution's business ethics. For example, when reflecting on his professional identity in stage 1, Damien said that he believes that education institutions should uphold high ethical standards to ensure that students' experiences are not exclusively the responsibility of the teachers. Rather, both the school and the teachers should share this responsibility and create a positive learning environment that yields success. This struggle appeared in other stages of his reflections as well, where he noted the teacher's responsibility in creating an interactive environment and his priority for interaction that may not always coincide with the institution's principles. In stage 3, theory, Damien reported that the primary concerns of his lesson-planning procedures are the goals and outcomes emphasized at his institution, but that he does not always follow them. Indeed, although Damien said that he tries to adhere to his institution's expectations to be a "successful teacher," he also observed that, when trying to comply with the "imposed standards," he tries to "make space" for his own beliefs. I never discovered the details of the various tensions he had with the institution beyond what I reported in Section 3.2.5, but apparently this tension never eased; he ended up leaving the institution.

Thus, I believe that we must acknowledge that engaging in reflective practice is not only a cognitive act/experience but also a deeply emotional one, and therefore we must consider how teacher reflections on their emotions and their social and professional sources can become more transformative for them as they seek to legitimize their practices within different organizations such as language schools. The findings of the case study presented in this Element suggests that in language teaching we may also need to discover more of an understanding about what Fook (2010, p. 49) has discerned as the "complex interplay of personally and organizationally experienced emotions" and how this can be incorporated into reflective teaching and learning. Fook has proposed that this understanding at the very least would involve finding out more about how the "emotional aspects of professional practice, both negative and positive, contribute to the making of professional identities and professional practices in particular workplace contexts" (p. 49). I believe that because the personal and professional are so intertwined, and Damien's professional identity and his professional practice clashed with those of his workplace, this may have led him to make a decision to move away from the workplace. However, I cannot be sure of this conclusion and thus we need to know more about how the subjective side of work can be better understood through the concept of reflective practice. I have attempted to incorporate emotions with the framework for reflection on practice so that we can encourage language teachers to become better informed and more self-aware of all aspects of their personal and professional relationships with colleagues.

Furthermore, as COVID-19 continues to disrupt all our lives, including language teachers who are now required to provide web-based lessons, we will need to learn more about how they reflect on these new online teaching experiences. The findings of the case study point out some changes such as the limitations of instructors' ability to easily provide critical nonverbal cues when students signal their understanding, which is easy to recognize in face-to-face instruction. This in turn makes it more difficult to interpret instructors' emotional experiences in an online environment. I used the Appraisal Framework to account for the emotional aspects of Damien's reflections so that he could develop emotional awareness. However, further research is needed that delves into language teachers' emotional reflections and how developing emotional awareness can help regulate their emotions to minimize stress especially in an online environment.

In terms of the utilization of the framework presented in this Element, Damien began his reflections in stage 1, philosophy, and moved through each of the five stages in sequence. This is similar to other case studies outlined in Farrell and Kennedy (2019) and Farrell and Macaplinac (2021). Such a deductive approach was chosen because Damien is considered an early career teacher (ECT) as he is still in his fifth year of teaching (Gordon, Kane, & Staiger, 2006). This theory-driven approach to practice where philosophy and theory have more of an initial influence on practice is probably a natural sequence of development for ECTs because they have not yet built up a repertoire of teaching experiences. When their early practices are observed, it is most likely that theory can be detected in their practice; however, over time and with reflection, it is possible that their everyday practice will begin to inform and even change their philosophy and theory and they may come up with new principles of practice.

However, teachers, teacher educators and researchers may decide to navigate a reverse process and take a more inductive approach to using the framework by moving from (beyond) practice into theory if they consider their practice (both inside and outside the classroom) as powerful determinants of their overall approach to reflecting on practice. For such an approach to the framework, teachers may first consider some issue from beyond practice (stage 5) or decide on a starting point from some issue within their classroom teaching that they want to explore, and then work their way through the different stages in reverse order. Indeed, it may have appeared that Damien went through each stage of the framework from stage 1 to stage 5 in something of a linear, lockstep fashion. However, what occurred was that Damien would include reflections on more than one stage at a time and would jump back and forth with reflections from different stages whenever an issue would bring him there. Thus, it is difficult to separate each of the five stages in the framework in reality, and although I reported each stage separately in Section 3.2, I also included relevant information from a previous stage if it had impact at another stage. For example, when reporting the findings of stage 5, beyond practice, I included Damien's reflections on his philosophy as stated in stage 1. Similarly, I would suggest future research be aware of the interconnectedness of each of the five stages and that no one stage is clearly separate from another.

Yet another way to navigate the framework was conducted by Playsted (2019) when she self-reflected on her development during her first year of teaching. She wrote journals and personal blog posts during her first year as a teacher and later used the framework as a lens through which to view and reflect on her writing during that year. While conducting her analysis, she also identified various critical incidents that she defined as "impacting events or personal interactions" (p. 42), which highlighted different stages of the reflective framework. Playsted pointed out that she did not move through the five stages in a linear process; rather her learning process was one of "looping back and forth (or framing and reframing a problem)" (p. 44).

In addition, after engaging in systematic reflection through the lens of the framework, the approach outlined in this Element encourages language teachers to take responsibility for their own informed decisions about what is important to them. As Fanselow (1988) has pointed out, "each of us needs to construct, reconstruct, and revise our own teaching" (p. 116). I believe that this is at the heart of reflective practice and I believe that language teachers can realize this by moving through the five stages of the framework presented in this Element, and make their own decisions about their practice, as demonstrated in the case study of Damien's journey through the framework. While I agree that it may be tempting to challenge Damien (I asked him to elaborate on many of his beliefs but did not challenge him on any) for example of the uses and abuses of his students' use of their L1 as a scaffolding mechanism, the origin of such a belief, and how that belief fits with his espoused language teaching and learning theories, I chose not to because I wanted him to reconstruct his own practice (or as Fanselow [1988, p. 128] put it, "the value of process, not product") and find his own truth. Had Damien asked me any questions about his reflections, which he did not, I would have provided my opinions. Such an approach to facilitating reflective practice that includes classroom observations takes on board conversations such as Fanselow (1988) suggests:

> Here I am with my lens to look at you and your actions. But as I look at you with my lens, I consider you a mirror; I hope to see myself in you and through your teaching. When I see myself, I find it hard to get distance from my teaching. I hear my voice, I see my face and clothes and fail to see my teaching. Seeing you allows me to see myself differently and to explore variables we both use. (p. 115)

In addition, administrators wishing to incorporate reflective practice in their workplace should be on guard against any top-down imposed form of retrospective reflections that can be interpreted either as opportunities to advance their particular agenda or as a remedy for difficulties in that workplace (Stark, Stronach, & Cooke, 1999). Such a top-down push to enforce reflective practice can backfire in that teachers can resent being used as excuses for a lack of resources or other such gaps in the organization's ability to develop a cohesive working environment. Such an implementation can be called, as Issitt (2003) pointed out, "deflective practice" and many who advocate such reflection "may not be skilled in its facilitation nor have the time or resources to support it" (p. 178). Institutions must allow for honest reflections by their teachers rather than top-down imposed reflections that institutions may use to get teachers to do what they consider is "good" or "quality" teaching, such as keeping their students happy, entertained, and/or passing exams.

Throughout this Element and in much of my other writings on the topic of reflective practice, I have noted that language teacher educators should always encourage language teachers of all ranges of experience to engage in reflective practice. I have also noted the difficulty in operationalizing reflective practice and I have provided a framework specifically for language that I believe can be a promising for all stakeholders interested in reflecting. I provided a case study of how a practicing teacher journeyed through the five stages of the framework with the aid of a facilitator, as discussed in Section 3.3. Although Damien's reflective explorations were presented as a kind of one-off event, I believe that language teachers should take a step back every so often (as Dewey noted) to systematically explore their practice either alone with the use of this framework (e.g., Playsted, 2019), with a facilitator, as in the case study outlined in this Element, and/or with a group of other colleagues (e.g., Farrell, 2014, 2016) for the purposes of continued professional development. Thus, I see reflection as a way of life. As Oberg and Blades (1990) maintain, reflection "lies not in the theory it allows us to develop about practice or reflection but the evolution of ourselves as a teacher. Its focus is life; we continually return to our place of origin, but it is not the place we left" (p. 179). I realize that some educators may not agree with my approach, but I hope that this Element will open up more possibilities for dialogue that further illuminates this fascinating, yet complex topic of reflective practice in language teaching.

5 Conclusion

The contents of this Element have suggested that we move beyond just citing Dewey and Schön's work to permit their use of reflection and consider the wider questions of what reflection is and how it should be operationalized for language teachers. Language teachers should not be "required" to reflect without any discussion beforehand on what they all consider reflective practice to be, or in whose tradition they are being asked to reflect. It is important, then, to allow time for language teacher educators, language teachers, researchers, and administrators to define and discuss reflection within their institutions, otherwise it will remain an ill-defined, intellectual exercise that is often reduced to a set of techniques that get done to fix perceived problems in practice. If such a stance continues with language teaching, there is a great danger of losing the real meaning of reflection as outlined in this Element, or, as Mann and Walsh (2013) noted, "a real loss of reflective spirit" where there is a total "disregard for teacher personality" (p. 293). As the Element indicates, I take a more holistic approach to reflective practice for language teachers that moves beyond but also builds on both Dewey's and Schön's important cognitive aspects of reflection by adding the spiritual, moral, emotional, or noncognitive aspects of reflection to the framework I presented. This holistic framework acknowledges the inner life of language teachers – who they are and what they stand for – and I believe this was demonstrated by Damien's reflections outlined in Section 3.2 as well as the analysis of his affective discourse throughout each stage. Though generalization is difficult to make from Damien's reflections and due to the inability to observe his teaching practices in person, there is every reason to believe that readers may find much of Damien's reflections has relevance for their own particular context, practices, and reflections. As Van Lier (2005) points out, rigorous analysis of a case study of just one teacher can provide in-depth insights into intricate pedagogical and contextual issues that "cannot be done adequately in any other common research practice" (p. 195).

I end this Element by defining my approach to reflective practice as a cognitive, emotional process accompanied by a set of attitudes in which language teachers systematically collect data about their practice and, while engaging in dialogue with others, use the data to make informed decisions about their practice both inside and outside the classroom. This definition builds on a previous version I suggested some time ago. I hope this Element provides a basis for language teachers, teacher educators, and administrators to recognize the possible transformational benefits of engaging in reflective practice within language teaching. I hope also that the additional detailed updated inclusion of the emotive aspects of reflection to the framework that I presented additionally provides a platform for others when operationalizing or practicing reflective practice so that we as a profession can provide the best possible learning opportunities for our language students.

References

Agudo, J. (ed.) (2019). *Quality in TESOL teacher education*. New York: Routledge.

Aguilar-Sánchez, J. (2005). English in Costa Rica. *World Englishes, 24*, 2, 161–172.

Akbari, R. (2007). Reflections on reflection: A critical appraisal of reflective practices in L2 teacher education. *System, 35*, 2, 192–207.

Anzalone, F. M. (2010). Education for the law: Reflective education for the law. In N. Lyons (ed.), *Handbook of reflective inquiry: Mapping a way of knowing for professional reflective inquiry* (pp. 85–99). New York: Springer.

Argyris, C., & Schon, D. (1974). *Theory in practice: Increasing professional effectiveness*. San Francisco: Jossey Bass.

Bartlett, L. (1990). Teacher development through reflective teaching. In J. C. Richards & D. Nunan (eds.), *Second language teacher education* (pp. 202–214). New York: Cambridge University Press.

Bleakley, A. (1999). From reflective practice to holistic reflexivity. *Studies in Higher Education, 24*, 3, 315–330.

Borg, S. (2011). Language teacher education. In J. Simpson (ed.), *The Routledge handbook of applied linguistics* (pp. 215–228). London: Routledge.

Boud, D., Keogh, R., & Walker, D. (eds.) (1985). *Reflection: Turning experience into learning*. New York: Kogan Page.

Boud, D., & Walker, D. (1998). Promoting reflection in professional courses: The challenge of context. *Studies in Higher Education, 23*, 2, 191–206.

Brookfield, S. D. (1990). *The skilful teacher*. San Francisco: Jossey-Bass.

Brookfield, S. D. (1995). *Becoming a critically reflective teacher*. San Francisco: Jossey-Bass.

Brookfield, S. D. (2009). The concept of critical reflection: Promises and contradictions. *European Journal of Social Work, 12*, 3, 293–304.

Burns, A. (2010). *Doing action research in English language teaching: A guide for practitioners*. New York: Routledge.

Campos, A. S. (2012). Teaching and learning English in Costa Rica: A critical approach. *Letras, 52*, 163–178.

Clandinin, D. J., & Connelly, F. M. (eds.) (1995). *Teachers' professional knowledge landscapes*. New York: Teachers College Press.

Coghlan, D., & Brannick, T. (2005). *Doing action research in your organization*. London: Sage.

Collin, S., Karsenti, T., & Komis, V. (2013). Reflective practice in initial teacher training: Critiques and perspectives. *Reflective Practice, 14*, 104–117.

Colnerud, G. (2015). Moral stress in teaching practice. *Teachers and Teaching: Theory and Practice, 21*, 3, 346–360.

Crookes, G. (2013). *Critical ELT in action: Foundations, promises, praxis.* New York: Routledge.

Cruickshank, D., & Applegate, J. (1981). Reflective teaching as a strategy for teacher growth. *Educational Leadership, 38*, 553–554.

Day, C. (1993). Reflection: A necessary but not sufficient condition for teacher development. *British Educational Research Journal, 19*, 83–93.

Dewey, J. (1933). *How we think: A restatement of the relation of reflective thinking to the educative process.* Boston: Houghton-Mifflin.

Ecclestone, K. (1996). The reflective practitioner: Mantra or model for emancipation? *Studies in the Education of Adults, 28*, 2, 146–161.

Edge, J. (2011). *The reflexive teacher educator in TESOL: Roots and wings.* New York: Routledge.

Edwards, G., & Thomas, G. (2010). Can reflective practice be taught? *Educational Studies, 36*, 403–414.

Fanselow, J. F. (1988). "Let's see": Contrasting conversations about teaching. *TESOL Quarterly, 22*, 1, 113–130.

Farrell, T. S. C. (1999a). The reflective assignment: Unlocking pre-service English teachers' beliefs on grammar teaching. *RELC Journal, 30*, 1–17.

Farrell, T. S. C. (1999b). Reflective practice in an EFL teacher development group. *System, 27*, 2, 157–172.

Farrell, T. S. C. (2001). Tailoring reflection to individual needs. *Journal of Education for Teaching, 27*, 1, 23–38.

Farrell, T. S. C. (2004). *Reflective practice in action.* Thousand Oaks, CA: Corwin Press.

Farrell, T. S. C. (2006). Reflective practice in action: A case study of a writing teacher's reflections on practice. *TESL Canada Journal, 23*, 2, 77–90.

Farrell, T. S. C. (2007). *Reflective practice for language teachers: From research to practice.* London: Continuum Press.

Farrell, T. S. C. (2008). *Novice language teachers: Insights and perspectives for the first year.* London: Equinox.

Farrell, T. S. C. (2013a). *Reflective practice in ESL teacher development groups: From practices to principles.* Basingstoke: Palgrave Macmillan.

Farrell, T. S. C. (2013b). *Reflective writing for language teachers.* Sheffield: Equinox.

Farrell, T. S. C. (2014). *Reflective practice in ESL teacher development groups: From practices to principles.* Basingstoke: Palgrave Macmillan.

Farrell, T. S. C. (2015). *Promoting teacher reflection in second language education: A framework for TESOL professionals.* New York: Routledge.

Farrell, T. S. C. (2016). *From trainee to teacher: Reflective practice for novice teachers.* London: Equinox.

Farrell, T. S. C. (ed.). (2017). *Preservice teacher education.* Alexandria, VA: TESOL Press.

Farrell, T. S. C. (2018). *Research on reflective practice in TESOL.* New York: Routledge.

Farrell, T. S. C. (2019a). *Reflective practice in ELT.* London: Equinox.

Farrell, T. S. C. (2019b). Foreword. In J. de Dios Martinez Agudo (ed.), *Quality in TESOL teacher education* (pp. i–iii). New York: Routledge.

Farrell, T. S. C., & Kennedy, B. (2019). Reflective practice framework for TESOL teachers: One teacher's reflective journey. *Reflective Practice, 20,* 1, 1–12.

Farrell, T. S. C., & Macapinlac, M. (2021). Professional development through reflective practice: A framework for TESOL teachers. *Canadian Journal of Applied Linguistics, 24,* 1, 1–25.

Farrell, T. S. C., & Tan, S. (2008). Language policy, language teachers' beliefs and classroom practices. *Applied Linguistics, 29,* 3, 381–403.

Fook, J. (2010). Beyond reflective practice: Reworking the "critical" in critical reflection. In H. Bradbury, N. Frost, S. Kilminster, & M. Zukas (eds.), *Beyond reflective practice: New approaches to professional lifelong learning* (pp. 37–51). New York: Routledge.

Freeman, D. (2016). *Educating second language teachers.* Oxford: Oxford' University Press.

Frenzel, A. C., Pekrun, R., Goetz, T., et al. (2016). Measuring teacher enjoyment, anger, and anxiety: The Teacher Emotions Scales (TES). *Contemporary Educational Psychology, 46,* 148–163.

Garton, S., & Richards, K. (2008). *Professional encounters in TESOL: Discourses of teachers in teaching.* Basingstoke: Palgrave Macmillan.

Gibbs, G. (1988). *Learning by doing: A guide to teaching and learning methods.* Oxford: Further Education Unit Oxford Polytechnic.

Gordon, R., Kane, T., & Staiger, D. (2006). Identifying effective teachers using performance on the job. Hamilton Project discussion paper. Brookings Institution.

Hargreaves, A. (2020). Mixed emotions: Teachers' perceptions of their interactions with students. *Teaching and Teacher Education, 16,* 811–826.

Harrison, J. K., & Lee, R. (2011). Exploring the use of critical incident analysis and the professional learning conversation in an initial teacher education programme, *Journal of Education for Teaching, 37,* 2, 199–217.

Hatton, N., & Smith, D. (1995). Reflection in teacher education: Towards definition and implementation. *Teaching and Teacher Education, 11*, 1, 33–49.

Hébert, C. (2015). Knowing and/or experiencing: A critical examination of the reflective models of John Dewey and Donald Schön. *Reflective Practice, 16*, 3, 361–371.

Hobbs, V. (2007). *Faking it or hating it: Can reflective practice be forced? Reflective Practice, 8*, 3, 405–417.

Holmes, M. (2010). The emotionalization of reflexivity. *Sociology, 44*, 1, 139–154.

Inforcostarica. (2000). Education in Costa Rica (html). Infocostarrica, January 17, 2001. Retrieved from www.infocostarica.com/education/educa tion.html.

Isenbarger, L., & Zembylas, M. (2006). The emotional labour of caring in teaching. *Teaching & Teacher Education, 22*, 1, 120–134.

Issitt, M. (2003). Reflecting on reflective practice for professional education and development in health promotion. *Health Education Journal, 62*, 2, 173–188.

Jay, J. K., & Johnson, K. L. (2002). Capturing complexity: A typology of reflective practice for teacher education. *Teaching and Teacher Education, 18*, 1, 73–85.

Johns, C. (1995). Framing learning through reflection within Carper's fundamental ways of knowing in nursing. *Journal of Advanced Nursing, 22*, 2, 226–234.

Killion, J., & Todnem, G. (1991). A process of personal theory building. *Educational Leadership, 48*, 6, 14–16.

Kim, H., Clabo, L., Burbank, P., & Martins, M. (2010). Application of critical reflective inquiry in nursing education. In Nona Lyons (ed)., *Handbook of reflective inquiry: Mapping a way of knowing for professional reflective inquiry* (pp. 159–172). New York: Springer.

Knezedivc, B. (2001). Action research. *IATEFL Teacher Development SIG Newsletter, 1*, 10–12.

Kolb, D. (1984). *Experiential learning as the science of learning and development*. Englewood Cliffs, NJ: Prentice Hall.

Kumaravadivelu, B. (2003). *Beyond methods: Macrostrategies for language teaching*. New Haven, CT: Yale University Press.

Lincoln, Y. S., & Guba, E. G. (1985). *Naturalistic inquiry*. Beverly Hills, CA: Sage.

Loughran, J. (2002). Effective reflective practice: In search of meaning in learning about teaching. *Journal of Teacher Education, 53*, 1, 33–43.

Lytle, S., & Cochran-Smith, M. (1992). Teacher research as a way of knowing. *Harvard Education Review, 62*, 447–474.

Mackenzie, C. (2002). Critical reflection, self-knowledge, and the emotions. *Philosophical Explorations, 5*, 3, 186–206.

Mann, S., & Walsh, S. (2013). RP or "RIP": A critical perspective on reflective practice. *Applied Linguistics Review, 4*, 2, 291–315.

Mann, S., & Walsh, S. (2017). *Reflective practice in English language teaching: Research-based principles and practices*. New York: Routledge.

Martin, J. R. (2000). Beyond exchange: Appraisal systems in English. In S. Hunston and G. Thompson (eds.), *Evaluation in text: Authorial stance and the construction of discourse* (pp. 142–175). Oxford: Oxford University Press.

Martin, J. R., & White, P. (2005). *The language of evaluation: Appraisal in English*. New York: Palgrave Macmillan.

Maxwell, J. (1992). Understanding and validity in qualitative research. Harvard Educational Review, 62(3), 279–301.

McCabe, A. (2002). Narratives: A wellspring for development. In Julian Edge (ed.), *Continuing professional development: Some of our perspectives* (pp. 82–89). Whitstable UK, IATEFL.

McGregor, D. (1960). *The human side of enterprise*. New York: McGraw-Hill.

MEP (2001). Programas de Ingles III Ciclo [English standards for Junior High Schools]. San Jose, Costa Rica: Ministerio de Educacion Publica.

Merriam, S. B. (2009). *Qualitative research: A guide to design and implementation*. Third edition. San Francisco: Jossey-Bass.

Merriam, S. B., & Tisdell, E. J. (2009). *Qualitative research: A guide to design and implementation*. San Francisco: Jossey-Bass.

Oberg, A., & Blades, C. (1990). The spoken and the unspoken: The story of an educator. *Phenomonology+Pedagogy, 8*, 161–180.

Playsted, S. A. (2019). Reflective practice to guide teacher learning: A practitioner's journey with beginner adult English language learners, *IJLTR, 7*, 3, 37–52.

Richards, J. C. (2013). Curriculum approaches in language teaching: Forward, central, and backward design. *RELC Journal, 44*, 1, 5–33.

Richards, J. C., & Lockhart, C. (1994). *Reflective teaching*. New York: Cambridge University Press.

Robbins, S. P., Judge, T., & Campbell, T. (2017). *Organizational behaviour*. Second edition. Harlow, UK: Pearson Higher Education.

Rodgers, C. R. (2002). Defining reflection: Another look at John Dewey and reflective thinking. *Teachers College Record, 104*, 4, 842–866.

Schön, D. A. (1983). *The reflective practitioner: How professionals think in action*. New York: Basic Books.

Schön, D. A. (1987). *Educating the reflective practitioner.* San Francisco: Jossey-Bass.

Shapiro, S. B., & Reiff, J. (1993). A framework for reflective inquiry on practice: Beyond intuition and experience. *Psychological Reports, 73,* 1379–1394.

Smyth, W. J. (1992). Teachers' work and the politics of reflection. *American Education Research Journal, 29,* 2, 267–300.

Spalding, E., & Wilson, A. (2002). Demystifying reflection: A study of pedagogical strategies that encourage reflective journal writing. *Teachers College Record, 104,* 1393–1421.

Stanley, C. (1998). A framework for teacher reflectivity. *TESOL Quarterly, 32,* 584–591.

Stark, S., Stronach, I., & Cooke, P. (1999). Reflection and the gap between practice, education and research in nursing. *Journal of Practice Teaching in Health and Social Work, 2,* 2, 6–20: 7.

Tabachnik, R., & Zeichner, K. (2002). Reflections on reflective teaching. In A. Pollard (ed.), *Readings for reflective teaching* (pp. 13–16). London: Continuum.

Teng, M. F. (2017). Emotional development and construction of teacher identity: Narrative interactions about the pre-service teachers' practicum experiences. *Australian Journal of Teacher Education 42,* 11, 117–134.

Thompson, N., & Pascal, J. (2012). Developing critically reflective practice. *Reflective Practice, 13,* 311–325.

Ur, P. (2020). Review: *The Routledge Handbook of English Language Teacher Education. ELT Journal, 74,* 4, 517–520.

Valli, L. (1997). Listening to other voices: Description of teacher reflection in the United States. *Peabody Journal of Education, 72,* 1, 67–88.

Van Lier, L. (2005). Case study. In E. Hinkel (ed.), *Handbook of research in second language Learning* (pp. 195–208). Mahwah, NJ: Lawrence Erlbaum Associates.

Wallace, M. (1996). Structured reflection: The role of the professional project in training ESL teachers. In D. Freeman and J. C. Richards (eds.), *Teacher learning in language teaching* (pp. 281–294). New York: Cambridge University Press.

Walsh, S., & Mann, S. (2015). Doing reflective practice: A data-led way forward. *ELT Journal, 69,* 4, 351–362.

White, P. (2000). Dialogue and inter-subjectivity: Reinterpreting the semantics of modality and hedging. In M. Coulthard, J. Cotterill, & F. Rock (eds.), *Working with dialogue* (pp. 67–80). Tübingen: Max Niemeyer.

Zeichner, K. M. (1983). Alternative paradigms of teacher education. *Journal of Teacher Education 34*, 3–9.

Zeichner, K. M., & Liston, D. P. (1996). *Reflective teaching: An introduction.* Mahwah, NJ: Lawrence Erlbaum

Zeichner, K. M., & Liston, D. P. (2014). *Reflective teaching: an introduction.* Second edition. New Jersey: Lawrence Erlbaum.

Zwozdiak-Myers, P. (2012). *The teacher's reflective practice handbook. Becoming an extended professional through capturing evidence-informed practice.* London: Routledge.

Acknowledgments

Thank you to the language teacher from Costa Rica and to Connie Stanclik for her reflections. Thanks also to George Jacobs for sharing his reflections and to the three reviewers of the manuscript for their careful reading and constructive comments. Finally, I would like to acknowledge the dean of the faculty of social science at Brock University for providing funds to help with this research.

Cambridge Elements ≡

Language Teaching

Heath Rose
Linacre College, University of Oxford

Heath Rose is an Associate Professor of Applied Linguistics at the University of Oxford. At Oxford, he is the course director of the MSc in Applied Linguistics for Language Teaching. Before moving into academia, Heath worked as a language teacher in Australia and Japan in both school and university contexts. He is author of numerous books, such as *Introducing Global Englishes*, *The Japanese Writing System*, *Data Collection Research Methods in Applied Linguistics*, and *Global Englishes for Language Teaching*. Heath's research interests are firmly situated within the field of second language teaching, and includes work on Global Englishes, teaching English as an international language, and English Medium Instruction.

Jim McKinley
University College London

Jim McKinley is an Associate Professor of Applied Linguistics and TESOL at UCL, Institute of Education, where he serves as Academic Head of Learning and Teaching. His major research areas are second language writing in global contexts, the internationalisation of higher education, and the relationship between teaching and research. Jim has edited or authored numerous books including the *Routledge Handbook of Research Methods in Applied Linguistics*, *Data Collection Research Methods in Applied Linguistics*, and *Doing Research in Applied Linguistics*. He is also an editor of the journal *System*. Before moving into academia, Jim taught in a range of diverse contexts including the United States, Australia, Japan, and Uganda.

Advisory Board

About the Series

This Elements series aims to close the gap between researchers and practitioners by allying research with language teaching practices, in its exploration of research informed teaching, and teaching informed research. The series builds upon a rich history of pedagogical research in its exploration of new insights within the field of language teaching.

Cambridge Elements ≡

Language Teaching

Elements in the Series

A full series listing is available at: https://www.cambridge.org/ELAT

Printed in the United States
by Baker & Taylor Publisher Services